Mrs. Alexander

What Gold Cannot Buy

A Novel

Mrs. Alexander

What Gold Cannot Buy
A Novel

ISBN/EAN: 9783744670852

Printed in Europe, USA, Canada, Australia, Japan

Cover: Foto ©Thomas Meinert / pixelio.de

More available books at **www.hansebooks.com**

WHAT GOLD CANNOT BUY

A NOVEL

BY

M<small>RS</small> ALEXANDER

Author of
'The Wooing O't,' 'Found Wanting,'
'A Woman's Heart,'
'A Choice of Evils,' Etc.

THIRD EDITION

LONDON
F. V WHITE & CO.
14 BEDFORD STREET, STRAND, W.C.

1896

Colston & Coy., Limited, Printers, Edinburgh

CONTENTS.

—o—

WHAT GOLD CANNOT BUY

WHAT GOLD CANNOT BUY

—o—

CHAPTER I

It was quite the end of the season, some
twelve or thirteen years ago, and for
some months the British public had break-
fasted, dined and supped full of the most
abundant crop of horrors ever supplied
to its readers by the busy pens of an
industrious press. The session had been
enlivened by animated debates on the
part England ought or ought not to
take in the war then devastating eastern
Europe, and bitter personal abuse levelled
at each other by contending orators

A

Now, politicians were counting the days till prorogation should set them free to use their tongues still more unscrupulously at county meetings and local dinners.

In the town residence of a wealthy widow, the Honourable Mrs Saville, Stafford Square, Belgravia, a note of preparation had sounded. The housekeeper had remarked to the butler that they had not too much time to get things ready before going down to the country.

Indeed, Mrs Saville had stayed unusually long in town, and, at the moment chosen to open this story, was sitting at the writing-table in her private room, a richly-furnished and luxurious apartment with yellow brocade curtains and stained-glass windows. She was a small, slight woman, with regular, delicate features, quick, dark eyes, and hair nearly white, combed back in the style that used to

be called *à l'Impératrice,* and surmounted
by a tiny cap of exquisite lace with a
tuft of scarlet velvet ribbon. The small,
thin hand which held her pen was loaded
with rings that flashed and glittered even
in the subdued sunshine, while the other
gently caressed the head of a small, silky,
pearl-coloured dog which lay on a chair
beside her.

She was speaking with a fair, large lady
about her own age, who occupied an arm-
chair at the other side of the table, and
who was rather gorgeously attired in out-
door dress.

"I am sure I interrupt you. You are
always so busy," said the latter, with a
comfortable smile, but showing no inclination to move.

"I do not mind being interrupted *this*
morning," returned Mrs Saville, not too
graciously; "my eyes are very tire-

some. They smart so when I read or write for any time. I really *must* get an amanuensis."

" Is it possible ? I should never suspect *your* eyes of being weak. They seem strong enough and sharp enough to see through anything."

" Thank you : they have served my purpose well enough."

" When do you leave town ? "

" I am not quite sure. I do not care to go until Hugh returns. He ought to be here now. This scare about trouble with Russia may bring him his appointment to a ship any day, and he ought to be on the spot. He has been ashore now for nearly a year."

" I wonder he chose the navy," said the visitor. " I should think the army must be much the most agreeable profession."

" My dear Lady Olivia ! who can account

for a young man's vagaries? My son is positively enthusiastic about his profession. He is very scientific, you know, and will, I have no doubt, rise to great eminence."

"Oh, I daresay he is very clever, but he is not a bit like other young men. I confess I do not understand him."

"No," returned Mrs Saville, with much composure, "I don't suppose you do."

"Not clever enough myself, eh?" said Lady Olivia, with a good-humoured smile. "Where is this bright particular star of yours just now?"

"When he last wrote he was still at Nice. He has stayed on there too long, I think. I trust and hope he does not visit Monte Carlo too often: I am not much obliged to Lord Everton for introducing Hugh to his gambling friends there."

"I don't fancy poor Everton's friends are generally what would be considered eligible acquaintances for the young and inexperienced, especially when they have pretty daughters who sing like angels— or prima donnas," she added, with a comfortable laugh.

"Pooh!" cried Mrs Saville, with a flash of anger in her keen black eyes, "Hugh is quite indifferent to all that nonsense."

"Is he? What an unnatural monster!" said Lady Olivia, rising. "I wish I could say the same of my George! However, he has taken to admire married women lately—which is a great relief."

Mrs Saville also stood up, and rang the bell. "Where is Everton just now? I want him so much to write to his cousin Captain Brydges on Hugh's behalf. I don't understand how it was

he did not do so before on his own
account."

"Oh, nobody knows where Everton is
to be found. He is coming to us in
September. We go down to Herondyke
on the 20th."

"Lady Olivia Lumley's carriage," said
Mrs Saville to the man who answered
the bell.

"Good-morning, then, dear Elizabeth.
Don't try your eyes too much. Shall we
meet you at the Montgomerys' to-night?"

"No; I am really sick of society."

"My dear, you must be seriously
ill!" cried Lady Olivia, with another
good-humoured but rather silly laugh,
and the sisters-in-law (which was their
relationship) shook hands, and parted.

Mrs Saville picked up her little dog
and took a turn up and down the room
with it under her left arm, a look of ex-

treme annoyance quivering in her eyes.
" What a fool that woman is !" she
murmured to herself; "not even a well-
bred fool! and to look at her, who
would imagine she was the daughter
of one earl, the sister of another? yet
there she is, started by the mere accident of birth in a position which cost
me all my fortune, my aristocratic marriage, my brains, to achieve. Still, I
do not complain : had these class distinctions not existed, there would have
been nothing to strive for, nothing to
attain. Still, Lady Olivia is a fool ; you
are a wiseacre to her, my precious
Prince," she continued, patting the dog's
head ; "you are a natural aristocrat; so
is Hugh, though he has some abominably
Radical ideas."

Here the footman opened the door,
and said deferentially, " If you please,

'm, Mr Rawson would like to see you."

"Yes, certainly Show him up."

In a few minutes the door again opened, to admit a gentleman, a short, stout, well-dressed man, slightly breathless, and apparently well braced up in his admirably-fitting clothes. His hair and complexion were of that neutral tint which is termed "pepper and salt," his eyes light grey and twinkling with a perception of the ridiculous, and his air, though it was politely respectful, showed a certain assured familiarity indicative of a confidential position.

"Well, Mr Rawson," said Mrs Saville, resuming her seat and placing her small favourite on the chair beside her, "what has brought *you* here to-day?"

Her tone was considerably more amiable than it had been to her previous visitor.

"What will, I hope, give you satisfaction. I fancy we will succeed in getting that piece of the Everton property you have been so anxious to purchase, for your price, and it will be a decided bargain. I am to see the vendor's solicitor finally on Thursday, when I fancy he will come in to our terms."

"I am very pleased, Mr Rawson; very pleased indeed. I must say, you always manage my business most satisfactorily. But you say several farms on the property are unlet. Now, I want my money to bring me in a decent percentage. What do you propose doing with the land?" Whereupon solicitor and client plunged into an animated discussion, in which Mrs Saville proved herself to be a shrewd woman of business.

"Well, Mr Rawson," she said, after

a short pause, "respecting a smaller matter, yet not an unimportant one. Have you made any inquiries about an amanuensis or companion for me?"

"I hardly thought you were serious in the wish you expressed—"

"I am exceedingly serious," she interrupted. "My maid who has just left me was really a very superior person, and could read aloud very well; now I have a totally different woman. I must have some one who is fairly educated, who can write, and keep accounts, and read French—I like French novels; she must be fit to associate with, yet ready to leave me to myself at a nod: I cannot be hampered with any one whose feelings I have to consider. She must have pleasant manners and a sweet voice, and look fit to be seen at luncheon and when she comes out with me."

"My dear madam, you have indeed set me a task! You must give me some time to find out such a treasure."

"I cannot give you much time. You must find her as soon as you possibly can. Advertise in all the papers; heaps of young women will apply; pick out one or two, but on no account let me be worried with an indiscriminate string of candidates: I know I shall be disgusted with them. I will not ask any of my acquaintances: they always recommend the most unsuitable people and are offended if you do not take their *protégées*. Then they bore you with pitiful stories. No, my dear Mr Rawson, let it be a purely business matter."

"I shall do my best. Suppose I try an advertisement in a provincial paper—"

"Do what you like; only remember I must have a presentable, well-educated,

well-mannered   young   woman—*young*,
mind, who will *save* me trouble, not
give me any."

"The labours of Hercules were a trifle
to this, the quest of the Holy Grail plain
sailing," sighed Mr Rawson.

"Oh, you will do it as cleverly as you
do everything. Now, tell me, have you
heard anything of my son lately?"

"Of which, may I ask?—Mr Saville?"

"No; of Hugh."

"Well, no, not for a week. He was at
Nice, I think."

"I know that, and it makes me very
uneasy. Why does he stay there? It is
not the season."

"Are you afraid of Monte Carlo? I
don't think you need be. Mr Hugh Saville
never was inclined to gamble."

"I am afraid of something much worse
—a designing woman."

" Indeed ? " And Mr Rawson glanced curiously at her.

" Yes," continued Mrs Saville, stroking the little dog's head thoughtfully. " When he was abroad some time ago (in the winter, you know) he made the acquaintance of a horrid old gambling, disreputable friend of Lord Everton's. This man has a daughter, and I heard accidentally that Hugh was a great deal with her. When my son returned I warned him against such penniless adventurers. He laughed in an odd, bitter way, and said, 'Don't trouble yourself, my dear mother : Miss Hilton would not look at me.' I at once saw some deep scheme in this : don't you ? "

" Well, I can't possibly say ; there are so many sides to human nature—feminine human nature especially. The young lady must be rather peculiar if she would not look at Mr Hugh Saville.

I should say he was rather a pleasant object."

"I know you are fond of Hugh, Mr Rawson; your regard for him strengthens the old ties that your excellent service has created."

"Humph!" said Rawson to himself, "does she think I am her footman?" "Yes," he observed, "your son was a true friend to my poor wild lad. It's owing to him that he is what he is now, and has a chance of a respectable life."

"I am very glad he was of use to your son," returned Mrs Saville, with an air of infinite superiority. "But, Mr Rawson, do you not think Hugh's answer evasive?"

"Mr Hugh Saville is never evasive. He may have been a little huffed with the young lady."

"Then she was on the track of some

other prey," said Mrs Saville scornfully. "I have an admirable match for Hugh, desirable in every way; so, when I found he had wandered back to Nice and was lingering there, I felt not a little uneasy."

"Did you say the young lady's name is Hilton?" asked Rawson, suddenly.

"Yes; her father is, or calls himself, Captain Hilton."

"Then I don't think you need distress yourself. I saw the death of a Captain Hilton about a fortnight ago in the *Times*. He died somewhere in France, but not at Nice. I noticed the name, because—oh, because I have heard Lord Everton speak of him."

"How can you tell if it be the same?" Mrs Saville was beginning, with great animation, when the butler appeared, carrying on a salver a large envelope bearing

the inscription " On Her Majesty's Service," and addressed to Lieutenant Hugh
Saville.

" This is some appointment for my son,"
cried Mrs Saville. " I knew it would
come in this unexpected way. Is it not
maddening that he should be absent ? "
As she spoke, she tore the letter open
and glanced at it, and exclaiming, " Yes,
as I thought ! " handed it to her confidential adviser. He took it, and read
as follows :—

" ADMIRALTY, WHITEHALL,
" *July* 20, 187—.

" SIR,—I have the honour to inform
you that you are appointed to H.M.S.
Vortigern, Flag-ship of Admiral Ward-
law, on the West Indian Station.

" You will proceed by the Mail leaving Southampton on the 26th instant
for Port Royal, Jamaica.

B

" If H.M.S. *Vortigern* has left, you will report yourself to the Senior Naval Officer, from whom you will get directions where to join your ship.

" I have the honour to be, sir,

" Your obedient servant,

" ROBERT BROWN,
" *Secretary to the Admiralty.*

"To Lieutenant HUGH SAVILLE,
"Stafford Square, S.W "

" There, that is just the opening Hugh has wished for—lieutenant of the flagship on the West Indian Station. Why, if this threatened rupture with Russia comes to anything, the West Indian Squadron would most probably be ordered to the Black Sea—*nothing* is more probable; then he might have a chance of distinguishing himself. I want to see my son an admiral! How infinitely provoking that he should be absent!"

"You must telegraph to him without a moment's loss of time," said Mr Rawson. "If he starts to-morrow, or to-night, why, he'll be here in thirty-six or thirty-eight hours — say Wednesday night or Thursday morning. Then he may have two days to get what he wants and catch the P & O. boat on Saturday. Very little time need be lost. Shall I wire for you?"

"Oh, yes, please; and reply to this, too. Let them know he is coming."

"Well, there is little danger of your son being caught *now*, Mrs Saville. If Venus herself had her hand on him he *must* break away, when such a summons may mean fighting. Good morning. Leave the telegram to me, and accept my best congratulations." Mr Rawson bowed himself out.

Mrs Saville mechanically rose and rang

the bell. Then she stood in thought for a minute, and rang again.

This time the butler presented himself.

"Atkins," said his mistress, "I expect Mr Hugh on Wednesday or Thursday. He will only stay to collect his luggage, and goes on to join the ship to which he has just been appointed. I want you to look out his chest and all his things. Let me know whatever you can see is wanting, and order the carriage immediately after lunch. Send Jessop to me."

"I really think I might as well go to the Montgomerys' this evening," she thought. "I feel so relieved, and even a glimpse of Hugh *en passant* will be delightful."

CHAPTER II

THE two ensuing days were full of excitement—pleasureable excitement—to Mrs Saville.

Her keen eyes shone with a hard glitter as she thought that her son was probably saved from committing some dangerous folly, and launched afresh on a career which promised honour and promotion. In truth, Mrs Saville's hopes and ambitions were centred on her second son. Her eldest was an apathetic, well-bred, briefless barrister, of dilettante tastes, given to writing elegantly-expressed papers, in the more exalted periodicals, on obscure passages in Shakespeare, and latterly in

Browning, on the derivation of obsolete words, and other such topics, in which ordinary mortals took not the slightest interest.

Mrs Saville was the only child and sole heiress of an exceedingly wealthy Sheffield manufacturer. She had married (not in her teens) the accomplished, amiable, distinguished-looking younger brother of the Earl of Everton, an impecunious peer, whose sole means of existence was derived from the rent of the family mansion and domains. Mrs Saville was an extremely ambitious woman; she had a keen desire for personal distinction, and in her own mind had resolved that as her eldest son must in the order of things succeed his uncle and become Earl of Everton, so Hugh must marry a woman of rank and fortune (whom she had already in her own mind selected for him), and thus she would be free to give the bulk of her belongings to support the title which would devolve upon her eldest son. He was a steady, irreproachable young man, but her heart, her pride, centred in her Benjamin.

Mrs Saville's love was a somewhat onerous obligation; she had a very tough, inexorable will, and a profound belief that she could manage every one's affairs considerably better than they could themselves—a doctrine in which her younger son rarely agreed. His mother's greed for power was greatly developed by her early widowhood, though the deceased Honourable, her husband, was a peace-loving soul who rarely contradicted her. Such was the condition of things at the beginning of this narrative.

Receiving no reply to her telegram, Mrs Saville sat up late on the following

Wednesday, hoping her son might arrive, and retired to rest weary with unfulfilled expectation.

When her maid brought her early cup of tea the following morning, she announced that "Mr Hugh arrived about half an hour ago, 'm, and has gone to his room."

Whereupon Mrs Saville ordered her breakfast to be brought to her in her own apartment, that she might not delay her son's refreshment, and prepared herself leisurely to meet him in her morning-room.

She was already there to greet him when he came upstairs.

" Well, my dear Hugh! I am glad to see you. My best congratulations. Have you read the Secretary's letter? I told Atkins to give it to you."

"Yes, he did," said Hugh, shortly;

then he kissed his mother's brow and stood looking at her with a troubled expression.

He was a fair, sunburnt man of perhaps six or seven-and-twenty, rather above middle height, broad-shouldered, and seeming shorter than he really was. His features were good, and a pair of large, handsome brown eyes lighted up his face, which was square and strong; his hair and thick moustaches were light brown, with a reddish tinge.

"Why, Hugh, you are looking ill and worn. Have you been ill?"

"No, not in the least; never was better."

"What is the matter, then? You do not seem like yourself. Why did you not arrive last night?"

"I came as quickly as I could: the trains at this season are inconvenient," he returned, still in an absent tone. He had a pleasant, deep-chested voice, and, though he had never given much time to its cultivation, could sing a good second.

"If you had started on Monday night after you had my telegram, you might have been here yesterday."

"I could not, mother." And he began to pace the room in quarter-deck style.

"Why?" persisted Mrs Saville, with vague uneasiness.

"Because I had a rather particular engagement on Tuesday morning."

"What do you mean?"

"I had arranged to be married on Tuesday morning, and I could not disappoint the parson and the consul, to say nothing of my *fiancée*," he returned, with a grim smile, and pausing in his walk opposite his mother.

"Married!" she repeated, growing white and grasping the arms of her chair. "Hugh! this is a stupid, vulgar jest."

"It is not, mother. I am married as fast as church and state can bind me. If I look haggard and seedy you need not wonder, for it isn't pleasant to leave your bride almost at the church door, I can tell you."

"Madman!" she hissed through her set teeth, while her keen black eyes flashed with fury. "To what adventuress have you fallen a victim?"

"Hush," he said, with some dignity; "you must not speak disrespectfully of my wife. To-morrow or next day you will see full particulars in the *Times.*"

"What!" she almost screamed, "are you in such haste to blazon your disgrace to the world?"

"I may as well let you know at once,'

he continued, not heeding her interruption. "My wife was Miss Hilton, daughter of the late Captain Hilton, an old cavalryman, of good family, I believe; but that I don't care a rap about."

"I expected this," said Mrs Saville, in a low, concentrated tone, and rising in her wrath. "Some inner voice told me evil would come of your long, unaccountable stay in that vile place. Now leave me. Never let me set eyes upon you again. You have blasted my hopes, you have destroyed my affection for you, you cease to be my son."

"Stop!" cried Hugh, in such a tone of command that his mother obeyed. "You must and shall hear me. Pray sit down. I have a good deal to say." He resumed his walk for a moment, while he strove to collect himself. Mrs Saville was silent, watching him with cruel, glittering eyes.

"You have a right to be angry," Hugh began, throwing himself into a chair near his mother's. "You have been a good mother to me, and you deserve that I should have consulted you — no, not exactly consulted, for a man has no more unquestionable right than that of choosing a wife, but that I should have told you in time of my intentions. Knowing that you would do your best to forbid or prevent the marriage, even to the length of writing cruelly to Kate, I determined to say nothing till the deed was accomplished. Now, hear me. I first met the Hiltons in Naples nearly two years ago, when I was with the Mediterranean Squadron. My uncle Everton was there, and I had leave now and again while we lay off Sicily. You know I never bothered about women, mother; but before I knew Kate Hilton a week,

I was fathoms deep. I don't know
whether other people think her beautiful
or not, to me she is the best and
loveliest—" Mrs Saville made a motion
of the hands expressive of disgust and
repulsion, while a contemptuous smile
curled her thin lips. "There, I will not
trouble you with details," continued
Hugh, grimly. "She sang—well, like
a prima donna, and she used to let me
sing with her, but the more I showed
her—well, the feelings I could not re-
press, the colder and more distant she
grew. She drove me half mad. Then
I was ashore, as you know, and went
off wandering abroad, hoping to meet
her, as I did. Still she kept me at arm's
length, but something told me that she
wasn't as indifferent as she seemed."

"No doubt!" ejaculated Mrs Saville.

"About six weeks ago, I went back to

Nice, and found old Hilton very ill—so bad that I could scarce get speech of Kate. They were lodging in the outskirts of the town. Then he died very suddenly at the last, and Kate, unnerved with watching and grief for the old man, who, though by no means a good father, was never actively unkind, broke down and clung to me. She was friendless, penniless, helpless. I took the command and insisted on her marrying me."

"Have you done yet?" asked his mother, harshly.

"Nearly. Have a little patience. As a woman, I ask you what opinion you would have of a man who could have deserted the girl he loved with all his heart and soul in such desolation? Could I have helped her, given her money, protection, anything, save as her husband? She was not her usual proud self. or she would have seen through the thin excuses with which I veiled your silence. Now, mother, be tender, womanly —ay, and reasonable. Make up your mind to the inevitable. Kate is my wife. See her before you condemn me, before you banish me. Give her the protection I cannot stay to give. I have left her with the kind old Frenchwoman in whose house her father died. I dared not endanger my career, my reputation, by losing an hour: so, for her sake as well as my own, I tore myself away. I don't think I ever asked you a favour: now I pray you, if you ever loved me, take my wife to your heart; let her live near you; give her a chance of winning your good opinion, your—"

A scornful laugh interrupted him. "Do you imagine I am as weak a fool as my son? such an abject weakling?

No, I shall have nothing to do with you or your wife. Go; I shall not see you again. You have never asked me a favour? Have I not paid your debts?"

"Yes, at old Rawson's request, not mine, nor should I have incurred them, had my allowance been measured by the needs and habits with which I had been brought up. My God! did you ever love my father, that you are so hardened against the first love of your son's life?"

"I had a proper affection for my husband, but I should never have forgotten myself for any man. I repeat it, you cease to be my son from this hour. You shall have the quarter's allowance now due to you, but after this not a penny more. See how you will get on with the beggarly pittance you derive from your father. To-morrow I shall see Rawson about altering my will. What wife will

c

compensate you for a life of poverty and obscurity ? "

"Poor we may be, but obscure, if I live, we shall not be," said Hugh, rising, and looking steadily at his mother, while he spoke very calmly. " I may deserve some censure for not informing you of my plans, but this treatment I do not deserve. And yet I believe you have a heart, though so calked and coated with worldliness that its natural impulses are hopelessly deadened, your natural good sense blinded to the relative value of things. What would the wealth of a kingdom be to me, if I knew the woman I love was groping her way painfully with a bruised spirit and bleeding feet through the rugged ways of life without a hand to help her? No, mother, your son is man enough to risk everything rather than that. I will obey you and go. Good-bye. God be

with you. I will never see your face
again, until you ask me and my wife
to visit you."

"Then it is farewell for ever," said Mrs
Saville, sternly. "Take my thanks for
this repayment of all the care and thought
and affection I have lavished on you."

Hugh stood half a minute gazing at
her, then, turning sharply, left the room
without another word.

Mrs Saville had risen to utter her last
sentence, and now walked to the fireplace
to ring sharply.

"Tell one of the men to be ready in
ten minutes. I want to send a note to
Mr Rawson. It requires an answer," she
said to the butler. "And, Atkins, I shall
not want you any more to-day : you had
better assist Mr Hugh. He is pressed
for time. I wish everything belonging
to him in this house to be packed

and removed by to-morrow evening at furthest."

"Yes, 'm," said the man, with a bewildered look, knowing that Mr Hugh was the favourite with his mother, as well as with the whole household.

"You understand me," said his mistress, sternly; "everything must be removed. And, Atkins, telegraph to Mr Saville. I think he has returned to his chambers, he was to be away only a week. Say I want him to come here to luncheon." The man, still looking stupefied, quitted the presence of his imperious mistress, who sat down to write with a steady hand and a curious, scornful smile on her lips.

Mrs Saville's son did not come to luncheon, and Mr Rawson's partner wrote his regrets that the head of the firm had left the office before Mrs Saville's note had arrived, and they did not know when

he would return, but that the writer
would wait on Mrs Saville at once if she
wished, and would telegraph.

So the obdurate mother's intention of
destroying her will at once was for the
moment frustrated. She therefore ordered
the carriage, and, after paying a round of
visits, took a long drive, reaching home
just in time to see Atkins inspecting a
pile of luggage being placed on a cab.
He hustled the men who were assisting
out of his lady's way, saying officiously,
as he did so, "We have nearly cleared
away everything, 'm. Just one or two
boxes are left for to-morrow. I did not
like to take them so late into a private
house, and it's a goodish step to Por-
chester Terrace."

"Do what you like," said Mrs Saville
coldly; "do not trouble me." And she
passed through the hall, thinking, angrily,

"So that weak-minded man Rawson is giving that miserable, ungrateful dupe, my son, shelter and encouragement. I will call him to account for this."

It was a wretched evening. Mrs Saville was to dine with a distinguished dowager, and with Spartan courage arrayed herself in her best and went forth to smile and utter bland nothings about her dear boy's haste to get off in good time, about his good fortune in being appointed to the flag-ship, and many more things about her mingled regret and satisfaction—polite inventions with which she vainly hoped to throw dust in the world's shrewd eyes.

Next day detection took the wings of the morning and came flying (if anything so solid could fly) in the shape of Lady Olivia Lumley. *Times* in hand, breathless, excited, she arrived before mid-day, a mark of unauthorised familiarity.

"Oh, my dear Mrs Saville, my dear Elizabeth, have you seen what is in the *Times?* I came off at once. I could not bear that any one should break it to you but myself." And she held out the paper doubled down at the fatal announcement among the marriages.

"No, I have not," cried Mrs Saville, savagely, snatching the paper, crushing it, and throwing it from her, "but I heard all about everything yesterday morning. I have disowned and banished my son. I will never see him again. But if you have come here to gloat over my rage and distress, you will be disappointed. I have merely cut off an offending member. He is not worth regretting. If you ever dare to mention the subject again, I shall decline to hold any communication with you or to give a reason for cutting you. The world can fill up the blanks."

CHAPTER III

MR RAWSON found even a warmer reception than he had anticipated awaiting him when he presented himself the following day in Stafford Square.

Bitter reproaches were showered upon him for his disloyal encouragement of an ungrateful son, a weak, contemptible dupe. But Mr Rawson defended himself bravely.

No one could do so much with Mrs Saville as the family solicitor. First, he was a shrewd, far-seeing man, of great experience and undoubted integrity, in whose judgment she had the greatest confidence. Then, too, he was a rich man and perfectly independent, both in position and in character. So high was her opinion of him that she deigned to call periodically on his daughters, and some years before, when she was in the habit of giving a large ball every season, sent them invitations, which were generally declined. Hugh Saville had been at school with the solicitor's only son, who was also in the navy, and, when the young fellow evinced a tendency to drink, stood by him and helped him at the turning-point where, but for friendly help, he might have taken the downward road.

Mrs Saville, though decidedly a *parvenue*, was too clever a woman to be a snob, though her love of power and distinction made her over-value the effect of rank and title upon her fellow-creatures. She was quite willing that her sons should be on familiar terms with Mr

Rawson's family; they were perfectly safe
in the society of his quiet, unpretending
daughters; while the sincere regard enter-
tained by Mr Rawson for the family of
his distinguished client, whose debts, diffi-
culties and involvements made many steps
in the ladder by which his father and
himself had climbed to fortune, lent something of a feudal character to the tie
existing between them.

To Mrs Saville the greatest power on
earth was money; to it she felt she owed
everything; but she was no miser. She
could be lavishly generous at times,
especially to any one who had served
or gratified her own precious self. She
could throw alms, too, to the needy, as
you would a bone to starving curs; but
to her the poor were not exactly men or
brothers. Yet, as her son said, she was
not without heart, only lifelong undisputed

command and unchecked prosperity had
hardened it; no one could do much for
her, or give her anything she had not
already, and amid the splendid sunshine
of her existence, one small cloud, " no
bigger than a man's hand," cast a deep
shadow against which her inner heart
rebelled. She was conscious that no one
loved her, except, indeed, her son Hugh.
This it was that made her so hard: she
did not realise that her manner, her
haughty aspect, repelled such sweet free-
will offerings as love and tenderness.

Hugh Saville was fond of his mother,
in spite of many quarrels he had inherited much of her pride and strength,
and a certain degree of sympathy existed
between them. When, therefore, he had,
as it seemed, thrown her over for a mere
clever adventuress, without a moment's
hesitation, the one tender chord in her

heart snapped, and a tigerish fury raged within her.

"My dear madam," said **Mr Rawson** when she paused in her reproaches, "I can quite understand your displeasure, but suffer me to suggest that I have a right to receive whom I like in my own house. I do not defend your son's imprudence; but, though you renounce him, surely you would not wish to deprive the poor young fellow of friends as well as kindred? You may be right in renouncing him, as an act of justice; to persecute him is revenge, and to that I will be no party"

"I do not understand these nice distinctions," cried Mrs Saville, "but I think your giving shelter to—to that disobedient boy is inconsistent with loyalty to me."

"Not in my opinion. Your son is not

the first young man who has left father
and mother to cleave unto his wife. He
has been singularly imprudent; still—"

"Imprudent! A dupe! a fool! an ungrateful idiot! Can't you see the game
of the adventuress all through?"

"I must say, such a construction might
be put on the disastrous story. If you
are right, however," continued Mr Rawson,
with an air of profound consideration,
"your son is more sinned against than
sinning, and our aim should be to cut
the fatal knot, if possible."

"Possible! Why, it is not possible.
The marriage is strictly legal."

"Nevertheless, if Mr Hugh Saville's
wife is the sort of woman you imagine
—and it may be so—she will hardly live
for a year and more away from her husband (the *Vortigern* will not be out of
commission for fourteen months at least)

—she will hardly live for all these months
alone, and within reach of the crew with
which her father used to associate, without getting into a scrape of some kind. I
propose to have her carefully watched. If
she gives us just reason for action, let her
be punished and your son saved from her
clutches. If she proves a good woman
and true, why, you must relax something
of your severity."

"I can safely promise what you will,
if she proves good and true. How do
you propose to find out?"

"The lady remains near Nice, in the
same rooms occupied by her father. Mr
Saville thinks that the owner of the house
is kind and respectable; his wife—well, I
must call her so at present—knows little
of English ways, and, besides, it is cheaper.
Now, there is a man already employed in
similar dirty work by an eminent firm

(not mine, I beg to say), and he can quite well accept a second commission ; only he must be warned not to find out what does not exist. We want facts, not condemnation."

"I want freedom for my son ; but the idea is a good one, Mr Rawson. I shall never be the same to Hugh, but I should prefer punishing the woman."

"It is but natural," remarked Rawson.

"At all events, I give you *carte blanche*. And remember, Mr Rawson, I *must* have my will to-morrow ; I am determined to destroy it. It strikes me that your coming without it to-day looks very like playing into Hugh's hands."

"You do us both injustice. I am reluctant you should change it, but your son never mentioned the subject to me. Indeed, he is too breathlessly busy, and a good deal harassed by his—by the lady's anxiety to come out as a public singer, for which she was trained. He—"

"For God's sake, no!" cried Mrs Saville, starting from her seat. "Anything but that! Great Heavens! imagine the name of Mrs Hugh Saville in huge letters at the top of a play-bill! It would be monstrous!"

"Oh, she would come out as Signora somebody I would not oppose it if I were you. But I think your son has forbidden the plan."

"Why should I take any further trouble?" said Mrs Saville, throwing herself back in her chair. "Let things go."

"Very well." Mr Rawson rose to take leave. "Lord Everton arrived yesterday. He makes some short stay in town, but no doubt he will call on you."

"Then I shall not see him. I shall get away, I hope, next week; I cannot

stay in town, yet I dread the country.
Do not forget to send my will this afternoon by a special messenger."

" I shall be sure to do so."

" And come the day after to-morrow to
take my instructions for a new one. I
don't wish to die intestate."

" My dear Mrs Saville, what a comic
idea ! "

" If you knew how I felt, you would
not think it an unnatural one. "

" A few weeks' quiet in the country
will set you up."

" The country, without companionship,
will not be cheerful; yet I want to get
away from every one. At Inglefield, however, I have my gardens."

" A delightful resource," said Rawson,
absently. His attention had begun to
wander, and he hastened to make his
adieux.

D

A conspiracy of small things, however, seemed to have been formed against the execution of Mrs Saville's plans.

Rawson faithfully fulfilled his promise, and sent her will, which that very night she tore up with vicious energy and burned in the empty grate of her dressing-room, but the trusty adviser was immensely engaged for the next fortnight, and when he offered the services of his partner they were invariably declined. Then, by some mistake, there had been a delay in beginning certain repairs and decorations at Inglefield (Mrs Saville's villa in Surrey), and when she drove down to inspect them she found the smell of paint so overpowering that she at once postponed her removal for at least ten days. Finally she sent for her doctor and commanded him to prescribe for the bad, feverish cold she declared she had

caught, and above all to order absolute
quiet. All this time her eldest son was
absent. He was spending a delightful
and profitable few days, which stretched
into a fortnight, with a learned antiquarian who had a place in Lincolnshire,
from where they enjoyed themselves examining the fine old churches to be found
in that shire, taking rubbings of brasses,
and spending happy mornings in decipher-
ing half-effaced inscriptions.

These were bitter days to the proud,
selfish woman, who felt that the love
which had kept her heart from freezing,
her nature from growing quite stony, had
been snatched from her by a stranger,
a mere adventuress, who most likely
saw in Hugh only a useful husband,
whose money and position would make
life luxurious and secure. For the sake
of this stranger, the son she loved so well

in her own silent, exacting way, had cast
aside all sense of duty, all affection, all
regard for her rightful authority. It was
the first check she had ever received, and
to her it seemed a moral earthquake.

The feverish cold she feigned at first
became really an attack of low fever,
and her medical attendant grew anxious
that she should have change of air.

Ill or well, she never ceased to insist on
having her new will completed and brought
to her for execution. In vain Mr Rawson
begged of her to await the return of her
eldest son and consult him first. Mrs
Saville rejected the suggestion with scorn.

"Richard knows no more about business
than one of his own chipped alabaster
saints. He has preposterous, unworldly
notions. I have no respect whatever for
his opinion, so just bring me my will
without further manœuvring. I know

you are working for that ungrateful, worthless son of mine; but it is of no use. If you refuse to do my bidding I can find plenty who will."

"Very true, Mrs Saville; but I do not deny that I am reluctant to see my young friend cut off without even a shilling. Do not be in a hurry. You cannot tell what time may bring forth."

"No, Mr Rawson, I will not wait. Death may come at any moment, and I could not rest in my grave if I thought that designing minx was revelling in the enjoyment of my money."

"Well, then, I will do your bidding. The day after to-morrow I will send my head clerk with the will. You can get one of your own people for a second witness."

"Then I shall leave town on Thursday. Until I have signed, sealed and delivered it into your hands, I shall not quit this house. Can I trust it to you, Mr Rawson?"

"My dear madam, do you take me for a felon?"

Mrs Saville smiled—a swift, bright smile, such as at rare—very rare—intervals lit up her grave face.

"Well, I shall leave it in your hands." There was a short pause, and she resumed : "Among all this worry, I suppose you have not had time to find me a lady companion?"

"Yes, I have made some inquiries, and find it is no easy matter. The fact is, I enlisted my eldest daughter in your service. She is a sensible, thoughtful young woman, and very anxious to select the right article. She was speaking to me only this morning, and was rather depressed about it. There are shoals of women seeking such an appointment, but very few that are suitable."

" One that did not suit would be worse than none."

" Exactly. Now, my daughter suggested something that might suit, if you do not mind waiting a week."

" I fear, Mr Rawson, I shall have to wait considerably longer."

" Well, the lady I was going to mention is the niece of our rector down in Wales, my native place. He has been dead many years, but this girl lived on with his widow, who died a few months ago. She is an orphan, very slenderly provided for, and is coming to stay with my girls for a few weeks. She is a gentlewoman, and well educated. I have not seen her since she was very young, so I will take a look at her before I say any more. If I think it worth while troubling you, she might call, and you could form your own judgment, or take her on trial for a couple of months."

" Thank you, Mr Rawson. I am very much obliged. I should like to see her, for I cannot have a fright or a dowdy before my eyes every day. When do you expect this girl ? "

" I am not quite sure. Soon, certainly "

" I should like to see her before I leave."

" I will ask my daughter to write this evening and ask her to come a little sooner."

"Yes, pray do. If she is at all reasonable and intelligent, she may be of great use to me. Imagine, Mr Rawson, Lady Olivia proposing to give me her 'dear Sophia' for six months, to be my daughter and to cheer me up! Why, the girl is as great an idiot as her mother !"

" Indeed ! The offer was well meant."

" I hate well-meaning people."

Mr Rawson laughed. " I suppose I

may tell you I had a few lines from Mr Hugh—" he began, when he was swiftly silenced by an imperative, "No, you may not. I will not allow that name to be mentioned before me, unless, indeed, we can succeed in breaking this unfortunate marriage."

Mr Rawson, looking very grave, bent his head.

"By the way, what is the name of the lady you mentioned?"

"Oh, Miss Desmond."

"Desmond does not sound Welsh."

"She is Irish on one side."

"Hum! I do not like Irish people."

"She is only half Irish."

"I could not have her reading aloud with that horrible accent."

"Well, is it worth while taking the trouble of seeing her?"

"Yes, I will see her," said Mrs Saville,

with decision. " I can tell at a glance whether she will do or not."

" Then I shall wish you a very good morning, and my daughter will let you know when Miss Desmond can wait upon you."

Mrs Saville thanked him again, and bade him a gracious good-bye.

CHAPTER IV

THE vindictive pleasure of signing her will, and receiving a stiff acknowledgment from Mr Rawson of its safe receipt, occupied Mrs Saville for a few days, before the expiration of which she received a few polite lines from Miss Rawson, saying that, if quite convenient, her young friend Miss Desmond would call on Mrs Saville between one and two on the following day.

"I am sure I hope she will do, and not be too silly," thought the imperious little woman, as she penned a brief acceptance of the appointment. "The generality of women are wonderfully foolish and narrow; though men are idiotic enough too, occasionally. A whole day of Richard's company is almost more than I can stand; yet he is always respectable, and would never commit the culpable folly his—there, I will not think any more of that."

The morrow came bright and warm, as befitted the last days of summer; and Mrs Saville established herself in the smaller of her two drawing-rooms, a beautiful and gorgeously-furnished room, full of buhl and marble-inlaid tables, luxurious chairs and sofas, old-china statuettes, flowers, and all the etceteras which wealth can give. It opened on a small conservatory in which a fountain played, and was cooler than her boudoir.

She was half reclining among the cushions of a lounge, with her precious little dog beside her, and trying to give

her attention to the *Times*, when the door
was opened and "Captain Lumley" was
announced.

"Why, where did you come from?"
she exclaimed, not too cordially, and
holding out her small, be-ringed hand
to a tall, slight, well-set-up young man,
with light hair and moustaches, laughing eyes, and a certain resemblance to
Hugh Saville, though of a slighter, weaker
type.

"From Herondyke, my dear aunt," he
returned, drawing a chair beside her. "I
have just a day or two in town, and I
thought I'd try if you were still here.
Deucedly hot, ain't it?"

"Yes, pleasantly hot. Are you on your
way to Hounslow?"

"Yes, just like my luck! they give
me my leave when there's not a thing
to do. And that young beggar Mignolles,

my sub, gets it next week, and will come in for the 12th."

"What a misfortune!" said Mrs Saville, sardonically. "I suppose you are all as usual?"

"Yes. Uncle Everton is at Herondyke just now, and in great force. He is the most amusing old boy I ever met. Are you better, Aunt Saville? My uncle said he called here on his way through, and you were not well enough to see him."

"I was not well; and I certainly should not get out of my bed to see Lord Everton."

"Wouldn't you? Well, I— Oh—ah— yes, to be sure," said the young man, hesitatingly, as he suddenly remembered his aunt's reason for wrath against the offending peer. "I am glad to see you looking so much better, at all events,"

he went on. " When do you go down
to Inglefield ? "

" On Saturday."

" I can often ride over and see you,"
continued Lumley, with a fascinating
smile. He had a nice voice and a pleasant, caressing manner ; indeed, he was
considered a very irresistible young man
by the women, and " not a bad fellow "
by the men.

" You are very good," frigidly.

" I suppose there is hardly a soul left
in town. Just called at the Montgomerys',
and found the house shut up : so I came
on here to have a chat and a bit of
luncheon."

" My dear George, I don't mean to
give you any luncheon. A lady is coming here ; she ought to be here now.
I am going to test her qualifications for.
the onerous office of companion and

' *souffre-douleur* ' to myself, and I can't have you here talking nonsense."

"By Jove!" exclaimed the young man, "this is quite a new idea!"

"Then, of course, it is strange to you."

"Won't she be a bore?"

"Do you think I shall allow myself to be bored?"

"Well, no, Aunt Saville," said Lumley, with a bright smile, "I don't think you will."

Here the door was again thrown open, and the butler announced with much dignity, "Miss Desmond."

"There, you may go," said Mrs Saville, impatiently.

"Very well," said the young man, good-humouredly. "I will call again before I leave town. My mother sent you her best love."

"I am very much obliged. If you

want a dinner, come back here at seven-thirty."

"A thousand thanks, I am already engaged. *Au revoir!*" He shook hands and retreated, pausing at the door to let a lady pass—a tall, slender young woman, in a simple black dress, as straight as it could be at that period of flounces, furbelows, draperies and sashes. The new-comer was young, yet youthfully mature; she wore a quiet, becoming bonnet, and was rather pale — warmly, healthfully pale — with wavy, nut-brown hair, a pair of dark grey or blue eyes, deepened by nearly black brows and lashes, a sweet, pathetic mouth and red, dewy lips; she moved with easy, undulating grace, suggestive of long, well-formed limbs.

"A deuced fine girl" was the young dragoon's mental commentary, as he stood

E

aside to let her pass, and, with a slight bow, disappeared from the room.

"Miss Desmond," repeated Mrs Saville, "come and sit here beside me." She looked piercingly at her visitor as she made a slight curtsey and handed her a note before taking a seat, saying, in a soft, clear, refined voice, "Mr Rawson was so good as to give me a few introductory lines."

"Quite right. A lawyer's instinctive precaution," returned Mrs Saville, opening it and glancing at the contents. "I suppose you know the usual sort of service expected from a companion? —reading aloud, writing letters, doing the agreeable when there is no one else to talk, and, above all, understanding when to be silent. It can't be the most delightful kind of life; but you will have a comfortable home if you stay."

Miss Desmond had coloured faintly while she listened, and now smiled, a pleasant smile, though her lips quivered as if she were a little nervous.

"When you want to earn your bread, you do not expect to be housed and paid merely to amuse yourself. I think I know what my duties would be."

"Add to this knowledge that I am a very exacting person, without a tinge of sentiment. I have no notion of treating any one who does me certain service for certain remuneration as a daughter. That is all nonsense."

"I think it is," said Miss Desmond, calmly.

Mrs Saville looked at her sharply, and met a pair of very steadfast eyes in which something like a smile lurked. "How old are you?" she asked, abruptly.

"I shall be two-and-twenty in September next."

"Hum! you look at once more and less than that. Can you read aloud?"

"Yes. Whether I can read well is for you to judge."

"Can you play or sing?"

"I can play a little—"

"I know what that means. Now, suppose you read me this speech of Lord Hartington's," handing her the paper. Miss Desmond took it, and immediately began. After about ten minutes Mrs Saville said, not unkindly, "That will do. You read fairly well. You do not pronounce some names properly."

"For names there is no rule, and sometimes opinions respecting them differ. I shall, of course, pronounce them in the way you prefer."

Mrs Saville was silent for a moment.

"If you are inclined to try a couple of months with me, I am willing to try *you*."

"That is best. Trial only can prove if we suit each other."

"Have you settled about terms with Mr Rawson?"

"Yes; they are most satisfactory."

"Very well. I shall go to the country in a day or two, and then I hope you will join me. You have been on the Continent, I believe, then you can read French?"

"Yes, fairly well."

"There is the bell. Pray join me at luncheon."

"Thank you, I shall be very happy."

"Takes things coolly," thought Mrs Saville; "knows her own value, probably. So much the better. I could not stand a gushing girl."

At luncheon the hostess started various

topics in an easy, unstudied way, and found that her young guest, though far from talkative, was quite equal to discussing them intelligently. As soon as they rose from the table, Miss Desmond took leave of her new lady patroness, promising to obey her summons whenever it came.

" Really," thought Mrs Saville, as she dressed for an afternoon airing, " I believe that girl may do. If she does not, why, it is no great matter. She certainly has the air and manner of a gentlewoman. '

Mrs Saville, however, was far too much preoccupied by her bitter reflections and vengeful projects to bestow many thoughts upon the new member of her household. But Miss Desmond received the expected summons in due course, and journeyed punctually by the appointed train towards her new home.

Inglefield, Mrs Saville's place, was scarcely an hour from Waterloo Bridge. It had, nevertheless, an air of seclusion not to be found at double the distance in other directions, the South-Western line, for some occult reason, never having found favour in the eyes of the smaller fry of city men. The picturesque country round Egham is comparatively free from the eruption of villa residences which crowd other localities.

Mrs Saville, who felt the quiet of her country home rather oppressive, began to wish for some one to break the painful monotony of her thoughts — some one whose face and voice were quite uncon- nected with the past—" the past," to her, meaning the ever-present image of her offending son. She had a certain sense of relief in the prospect of companionship, for in truth she was, and always had been, a very lonely woman. When, therefore, shortly before dinner, Miss Desmond arrived, she was received with comparative cordiality.

" I told them to send down the omnibus, as it would be more convenient for your luggage," said Mrs Saville, after they had exchanged greetings.

" My luggage consisted of one dress-basket," said Miss Desmond, smiling. "Considering that my stay may be but short, I did not like to bring more."

" That was prudent. Now I am going to dine early—that is, at six—in order to take a drive afterwards : the evenings are the best part of the day."

That first evening was trying. Mrs Saville was very silent, but so long as they moved smoothly and rapidly through cool, dewy woods, fragrant fields, and gently-winding lanes with rustic fences

and picturesquely-broken banks, the silence
was not oppressive. Miss Desmond had
plenty to think of—the struggles and diffi-
culties of youth spent in genteel poverty ;
the loss of her nearest and dearest; the
vanishing of many a dream that even at
twenty-two life had taught her must be
resigned ; and through all, the enduring hope which in such strong natures
is too deeply rooted to be scorched by
the noontide heat or withered by the
midnight blast—the instinctive conscious-
ness of her own tenderness and loyalty,
which gave vitality to her belief in the
possibility of happiness. The quiet beauty
of the country, the soothing tranquillity
of the hour, gave her an exquisite
sense of rest which she thankfully
accepted.

Returned, however, and shut up in the
lamp-lit drawing-room, silence did become

oppressive, and Miss Desmond, remember-
ing her employer's hint, felt reluctant to
break it.

"I suppose you do needlework? Girls
like you generally have something of that
kind in their hands."

"I do a good deal, and I have some
that can appear in a drawing-room.'

"I used to do fancy-work myself," said
Mrs Saville, "for it is intolerable to sit
idle; but I find I dare not trifle with my
eyes, which I have always tried too much.
However, I must do something. I cannot
sit with my hands before me while you
read."

"Knitting is not bad for the eyes,"
suggested Miss Desmond.

"I have always despised it as purely
mechanical, but now I shall be obliged to
adopt it. Do you know how to knit?—
can you teach me?"

"Yes; I did a good deal of knitting when I was in Germany."

"Oh! do you understand German?'

"I could make my way in Germany; but I cannot read German aloud as I do French."

"And I do not understand a word of the language. I was only taught French and Italian. Ah, what a potent epitome of mankind's opinion, the rage for that uncouth tongue as soon as the race that speaks it succeeded! Success is the measure of everything."

"I cannot think so. We have no plumb-line with which to fathom the depth where future triumph lies hidden under present failure."

"That is no argument," returned Mrs Saville. "Now, Miss Desmond, I am going to my room, and I dare say you will be glad to do the same. I breakfast in summer at eight. Good-night."

The next few days enabled Mrs Saville and her newly-established companion to fit into their places. " She is less formidable than I expected," thought the latter. " I must keep constantly before my mind that she is on her trial with me, as I am with her. I am not bound to spend my life here, nor have I given up my freedom. She interests me ; for, hard as she seems, I believe she is not without heart. Shall I ever be able to find it ? "

" That girl is not so tiresome, after all. Thank heaven, she is no fool, and she is not a bit afraid of me," mused Mrs Saville. " How I hate and despise folly and cowardice ! they generally go together. There's a great deal of style about her, yet she must have been always steeped to the lips in poverty. If I had a daughter like her I should want the first statesman in England for

her husband. Bah! what folly! If I had
had a daughter she would have been as
indifferent to me as the rest, and would
probably have married a groom to spite
me. As no one cares for me, I had
better concentrate my affections on myself. People may be indifferent to love,
they are never indifferent to power; and
money is power, especially if backed by
common sense."

So the knitting and reading went on
successfully, and Mrs Saville was sometimes surprised by the light-hearted enjoyment which her *lectrice* showed in any
drolleries which cropped up in the course
of their readings. Mrs Saville herself
was not without a certain grim sense of
humour, but she was sometimes surprised,
and not too well pleased, at the quick
perception of the ridiculous which so
often gleamed in Miss Desmond's expres-

sive eyes. Laughter is what neither
pride nor power can defy, and few can
hope to impose on him or her whose instinctive feeling of the absurd can blow
away the chaff of pretension. Still, to her
patroness the young lady's manner was
not only perfectly well bred, but tinged
with a sweet deference which implied a
willingness to do her service which did
not fail to please the stern woman, while
it in no way touched her self-respect.

Miss Desmond had been little more
than a week at Inglefield, when, returning home from the neighbouring vicarage
whence she had been despatched with a
message respecting some of the local
charities to which Mrs Saville contributed,
she entered the drawing-room through one
of the French windows which opened on a
verandah and thence on to the grounds.

The lady of the house was not there,

but lounging comfortably in her especial chair sat a gentleman, who, directly Miss Desmond entered, rose and made her a bow—a bow which proved that bowing was not yet quite a lost art. He was a tall, elderly man of uncertain age, slight and elegant, with fine, aquiline features and light-blue, laughing eyes that looked as if boyhood still lingered there in spite of the wavy grey hair that curled round a rather low but well-shaped forehead. He was carefully, admirably dressed, and indescribably fresh and cool, though it was a burning August day.

"Allow me to explain my appearance here," he said, in a pleasant, youthful voice. "I have taken the exceedingly uninteresting journey from London to this villeggiatura, and I now await its amiable mistress's pleasure as to whether she will see me or not."

"Has she been told you are here?" asked Miss Desmond, taking off a large garden-hat, which she continued to hold in her hand, wondering who this could be. Mrs Saville's visitors had hitherto been few and far between, her acquaintances at that season being scattered in remote regions.

"Yes, I believe her major-domo has conveyed my pasteboard to the august presence." And the stranger, with the air of being very much at home, drew forward a chair, which Miss Desmond did not accept.

"Pray, has Mrs Saville been long here?"

"About a fortnight."

"And you—have you been here all that time?"

"Not quite."

"Ah! what wonderful resisting power!

I should have imagined you would both by this time be extinct from mental inanition." Miss Desmond laughed—a sweet, well-amused laugh.

"And you can laugh like that!" he continued. "Then your vitality has of course kept my revered sister-in-law alive. It must, however, exhaust your own vital powers to give out ozone—no, what do they call it?—electricity—to such a degree. There is nothing to me so soul-destroying, so deadening, as suburban rusticity. Won't you sit down? I can't stand any longer myself."

"Then pray do not. I do not sit down because I am not going to stay. I thought Mrs Saville would come in immediately," said Miss Desmond, who began to perceive in some way that this pleasant, talkative personage was a good deal older than he seemed.

F

"Since you permit it, then." And he sank into his chair with a sigh of relief.

"You see," he went on, "this sort of place is just far enough from London to cut you off from all the conveniences of town life, and too near for any of the legitimate amusements and occupations of the country. Why, if you did flush a partridge you dare not let fly at him, for fear of your neighbour's cocks and hens!"

"As I never hunt or shoot, this seems a most delightful abode to me," she returned, smiling.

"By Jove! you are easily pleased," said he, looking rather earnestly at her. "By the way, I do not think I have had the pleasure of meeting you before; indeed, I am sure I have not, for I could not possibly forget you!" Miss Desmond made him a pretty, saucy curtsey.

"Couldn't, 'pon my soul! So I fear I
have not the honour of counting you
among my kinsfolk."

"Indeed you have not," laughing a
sweet, fresh laugh. "I am Mrs Saville's
demoiselle de compagnie, and am paying
her a probationary visit."

"The deuce you are! What immense
courage some women have!—though they
say the race of Amazons is extinct."

Here the butler appeared, and said,
"Mrs Saville will see you, my lord, if
you will come this way." The gentleman
rose, and made another elegant bow as he
passed Miss Desmond, saying in a low
tone, "Pray for me, sweet saint!" and
left the room.

"What an amusing person! I wonder
who he is. Some relation, I suppose, or
he would not speak so freely," thought
Miss Desmond. "I must not go to Mrs

Saville at present." She too left the
room by a different exit, and ascended to
her own pleasant apartment, which looked
out to the front ; a dressing-closet opened
from it, and, except for the bed, it was
furnished like a sitting-room. After leaning from the window for some minutes,
apparently in deep thought, she went to
her writing-table, and, unlocking a desk
with a key which hung to her chain, she
began to add some lines to a closely-
written letter which lay therein.

She had written for a considerable time,
when the sound of wheels and horses' feet
drew her to the window, from whence
she saw the gentleman with whom she
had spoken in the drawing-room descend
the hall door steps to enter a very rusty
fly or station cab. He had a comically
rueful expression of countenance, and,
looking round over the front of the

house, his quick eye caught sight of Miss
Desmond. To her annoyance, he lifted
his hat and gave a slight, expressive shrug
before stepping into his cab, which drove
off immediately.

"I wish I had not looked out," she
thought; then, smiling at the idea, it
struck her as very like an "expulsion."
"No doubt Mrs Saville could be very
severe—even cruel, but she is good to
me. I had better give her the vicar's
message; yet I feel half afraid. This
will not do. My best, my only chance
is fearlessness."

She paused a moment, then locked
away her writing again, and proceeded
down a long passage and a short stair
to the wing in which was Mrs Saville's
study. (The word boudoir is quite in-
appropriate.)

She knocked at the door, and was

imperatively told to come in. Mrs Saville
was walking up and down, evidently
much disturbed.

"I beg your pardon," hesitating.

"Oh, come in, come in! I have been
worried by an importunate fool; but I
am not so overset that I cannot attend
to anything else. Did you see the
vicar?"

"I did; and he is very sorry, but he
has already returned the plans of the
cottages to the builder."

"Then he must get them back," very
sharply. "I will walk over myself to
the vicarage. I want movement, and
Prince wants a walk." She sat down
as she spoke, and took her little dog
(which was begging for Miss Desmond's
notice) on her lap. "Did you happen
to see Lord Everton?"

"The gentleman who has just left?

Yes; he was in the drawing-room when I came in."

"He is one of the most contemptible men in England," continued Mrs Saville —"a mere butterfly at sixty-three. He has only existed for pleasure his whole life, and even now pleasure still pleases. His sense of enjoyment has been his ruin. A trifler of the most trifling description, without an ambition or an aim, worst of all, reckless of how he may throw others into temptation or difficulty. He has injured *me* past forgiveness, and yet he comes meandering here to try and talk me over to induce me to pardon the cruellest injury that could be inflicted. I told him my opinion fully; but to be seriously angry with such a creature is like taking a howitzer to shoot a humming-bird. Come, Miss Desmond, let us go out into the open air. What o'clock is it ? Nearly five ? I shall walk round the grounds until it is time to find the vicar."

They paced somewhat slowly across the grounds to a wooded rising ground on the left of the house, from which a view of it and its surroundings could be obtained, and when they had accomplished the ascent Mrs Saville sat down, as if tired, on a seat placed at the best point of outlook. Her companion had observed that the keen, active woman was stronger in spirit than in flesh, and felt a sort of pity for this rich, prosperous, desolate lady.

"What a sweet, beautiful place this is !" she exclaimed, after gazing at the scene before her for a few minutes. " I think it is the most charming I have ever seen."

"Then you have not seen much," returned Mrs Saville, testily.

"That is true. I have not seen any fine places in England, and the palaces and châteaux abroad are so melancholy; but who could desire anything beyond the exquisite, graceful, home-like beauty of Inglefield?"

It was, in truth, a delightful abode, sheltered on the east by the upland from which they now looked down; the ground sloped steeply from the opposite side, giving a wide view over a richly-wooded country; while the house, gardens and grounds occupied the level space between. Fine trees stood about, for Inglefield was an old country-house dating tolerably far back, built in the half-timbered style, the first storey of fine bricks, the upper part beams and plaster, with high chimneys and many-gabled roofs. The large additions made by Mrs Saville's father had been carried out in strict accordance with

the original plan, and the garden de-
signed to suit it also.   A circular lawn,
surrounded with flowering shrubs and
dotted with several large, spreading trees,
separated the house from a wide avenue
which opened exactly opposite the entrance, overarched by a double row of
great old elms at either side.   Beyond,
on the left, from a wooded hollow, through
which a trout-stream had been widened
and dammed into a miniature lake, glimpses
of which could be caught when the sun-
light fell upon it, rose the smoke from
some unseen chimney.

"Home - like," repeated Mrs Saville.
"There is an immense amount of nonsense talked about home.   I wish you
could see Kingswood, Lord Everton's
place; it is one of the finest seats in
England — full of family treasures and
historic relics — and he would not make

the faintest effort to retain it. He might have entered diplomacy, or taken a foreign appointment and saved money. But he is quite content to derive his income from the rent a Manchester millionaire pays him for his ancestral halls, when he might have married the millionaire's daughter and kept it for himself."

"Well, if the daughter was not the sort of woman he could love, he was right," said Miss Desmond, thoughtfully. "Suppose she was not companionable, that he could not love her; the finest place in the world could not make up for that."

"You are a foolish child! The thing called love soon evaporates. Rank, importance, high position, last, and duties due to one's station fill up life satisfactorily. It is a low, mean conception of existence to spend it in personal pleasure."

" Yes, certainly. You are right," eagerly. " To live for one's self alone, in any way, is miserable. But one has a right to try and be happy if it does not interfere with the happiness of others."

" You have been tolerably poor, from what you say," said Mrs Saville, not unkindly. " Have you been happy ? "

Her interlocutor paused before she replied, " Yes, on the whole I have been happy. Sometimes it has been trying to feel shabby and to be unable to get a new dress, to know that lovely pictures and delightful music were within your reach, yet inaccessible for want of a few francs; still, when I *could* have the dress, or see the pictures, or hear the opera, it was heavenly. The worst is to want nice, delicate things for some one you love and not to be able to get them ; that *is* bitter,

Still, nothing can be so poverty-stricken as to have no one to trouble about, no one to love or live for, no one to love *you*."

"It is, then, very unfortunate for a person of your disposition to have lost your home," remarked Mrs Saville, coldly.

"It is sad enough; but I have been fortunate in finding friends like Mr Rawson and his daughter. It is better, too, to believe that there is some pleasant, sheltered nook round the next turn of the road than always to look for sandy deserts. Loneliness is the worst evil of all: it is what I fear most."

Mrs Saville did not answer immediately; then she said abruptly, "What is your name—your Christian name?"

"My name? Hope Desmond."

"I thought so. It is very appropriate. You have given me a curious mental picture. I suppose it is true, though it is incomprehensible to me, but you give me the idea of being sensible and accurate. Do you not feel that your life has been lost, fruitless, passed as it has been in this constant struggle?"

"No," cried Hope, her dark eyes lighting, and lifting her head with an unconscious but dignified movement. "It has had much sweetness, and I have been of some use. Though I am not clever, I have done what I could; and that will always comfort me. I do not fear the future. Work will come to me. I would not change with any one. I prefer to remain the 'me' that I am."

"You are an unusual specimen, Miss Desmond, and really a profound philosopher; yet you have refinement and taste, ay, and culture enough to enable you to enjoy beauty and elegance, literature and

art.   I congratulate you ; only, if *every*
one was as easily pleased the world would
stand still."

" Perhaps so," said Hope Desmond, with
a sigh.   " I can only see life according to
my lights."

Then, after some minutes' silence, she
observed how prettily the smoke curled
up from among the trees down in the
hollow.

" Yes," said Mrs Saville, " I suppose
Lord Castleton has arrived.   Inglefield
Court belongs to him.   It is an older and
much damper place than this.   I must
call to-morrow."   She heaved a deep sigh
as she spoke.   " Miss Dacre is one of the
fortunate ones, according to *my* estimate.
She is her father's sole heiress, and takes
the title, too, when she succeeds him.   She
is rather pretty, rather accomplished, and
decidedly popular.   I used to see a good

deal of her at one time; now—" She paused and frowned, then, rising, she said, peremptorily, "Come, I feel rheumatic: I have sat here too long. Where is Prince? Call him, please; he gets lost in the underwood when he tries to hunt about as if he were a big dog."

Hope dived among the bushes and recovered the little truant, bringing him back in her arms, the creature making violent efforts to lick her face all the way.

Few words passed between the companions till almost at the gate which opened from Mrs Saville's grounds on a footpath which crossed the vicarage fields, when that lady said, suddenly,—

"I expect my son to-morrow."

"Your eldest son?"

"I have but one son," returned Mrs Saville, icily; then after a moment's pause she exclaimed, " Do take Prince up and give him to me : there is a cow at the end of the field, and the little spitfire is sure to attack it ! "

CHAPTER V

RICHARD SAVILLE was not a favourite with his mother, though he had never given her the least trouble. He was a tall, slight young man, but there was no dignity in his height, for it was neutralised by a stoop conveying the impression that he had not strength enough to hold himself upright. He had dark hair, rather thin about the temples, and well-shaped brown, but evidently short-sighted, eyes; his manners were cold, though gentle, and he gave a general impression of languid circulation and extreme correctness. He had inherited something of the Saville indifference to everything save his own peculiar

98

tastes or fancies, and a good deal of his uncle Everton's obtuseness as regarded personal distinction.   His keen-sighted mother soon perceived that her first-born would never fulfil her ambitious aspirations, and this contributed to her strong preference for her younger son, on whose career she had built her hopes, though his choice of a profession had greatly annoyed her. Hugh had inherited all the plebeian energy which made his maternal grandfather a wealthy and useful member of the community, and he cared little for any personal distinction not earned by himself.   Nature intended him for a radical, and the accidents of birth and early association gave him certain aristocratic leanings—which conjunction of centripetal and of centrifugal attraction made him a tolerably round-minded man.

He and his brother were excellent

friends, in spite of the low estimate each had of the other's tastes.

The arrival of Richard (no one ever dreamed of calling him Dick) was, on the whole, an agreeable change in the routine of life at Inglefield. He soon discovered that Hope Desmond was a sympathetic listener; he therefore confided to her the great scheme he had conceived of compiling a book to contain all the English phrases and proverbs that were distinctly derived from the Anglo-Saxon, and he soon grew sufficiently familiar to ask if Miss Desmond would be so good as to assist him in his work, whenever his mother could spare her.

" I will do so with pleasure, Mr Saville," she returned, in her frank, fearless way. " But you must ask your mother's permission, and before me. She is a person not to be trifled with."

" I know that," he said, hastily, "and
I will do so on the first opportunity."
Which he did, in a nervous, hesitating
way.

" Who cares for Saxon phrases ? " replied
Mrs Saville, contemptuously. " Miss Desmond would be more usefully employed
making flannel petticoats for my poor old
women. However, if she chooses to bestow some of her spare half-hours on your
investigation of such a dust-heap, I am
sure she has my consent."

Hope Desmond's time was pretty well
occupied, for she had come to be secretary
as well as companion to her active
employer : still, she gave Richard Saville
what parings of time she could, and, if
occasionally bored, was not a little amused
at the profound importance he attached
to his work.

But Richard Saville's presence entailed

other changes.   Captain Lumley found it
suited him to ride over very often to
luncheon, and sometimes to dinner, staying the night, almost without a distinct
invitation from the hostess, who seemed
to think two such fledglings beneath her
notice.   Young Lumley did his best to
attract Hope's notice, and flattered himself that she smiled upon him.

"So you have really managed to survive—how long ?—five weeks under my
aunt's jurisdiction ?" he said, having discovered Hope with a book in her hand
in one of the shady nooks of the garden
one day after luncheon.

"I have, and without any difficulty,"
she returned, making room for him on
the seat beside her, as she greeted him
with a kindly smile.   He threw away his
cigar, and readily accepted the place, thinking be had already made an impression.

"Mrs Saville has been very nice and pleasant. If she were not I would not stay."

"Pleasant! Come, that's a little too much. She is an uncommon bright woman, I know, but it's in the flash-of-lightning style, and lightning sometimes kills, you know."

"Well, she hasn't killed me."

"No, I fancy you take a great deal of killing. Perhaps that's because you are so killing yourself."

"Oh, Captain Lumley! that is a style of compliment a *commis-voyageur* might offer to a barmaid. It is not worthy of a gallant—what are you?—hussar?" said Hope, laughing good-humouredly.

"You have taken a leaf out of Mrs Saville's book," cried Lumley, while he thought, "What teeth she has — regular pearls, by Jove!' "If you are as hard on me as she is," he continued aloud, "I shall not be able to live here."

"I suppose you are not obliged to stay?"

"Well, no; but I do not like to go away."

"Then you must strike a balance," said Hope, and rose up as if to return to the house.

"What! are you going in? It is ever so much nicer here."

"I shall go through the wood to the glebe gate."

"And may I come?"

"Oh, yes, if you like. Here, Prince, Prince!"

Lumley felt a little at a loss what to say next. "I suppose you have the care of that small brute?"

"No; I have the privilege of taking him out, and I am very fond of him."

" Well, he is rather a nice little creature. He never snaps at me."

" He is a very compassionate, forbearing doggie," said Hope, raising her laughing eyes to his.

" Thank you, Miss Desmond. So you are going to help my cousin Richard with his—dictionary—what do you call it ? "

" I really do not know what its name is to be. Yes; if I can find time I will do some writing for him."

" Richard has more sense than I thought."

" At all events he is desperately in earnest, and that is always respectable."

" Exactly : that is just what he is."

A pause ensued, broken only by Prince barking violently at some sparrows, which totally disregarded him.

" Miss Dacre is coming to dinner, and the vicar and vicaress."

"Oh, indeed!" said Hope.

"Miss Dacre is rather pretty for an heiress, and rather a jolly girl. You'll like her."

"Very probably, were I to meet her; but I shall not dine with you."

"No? What an infernal shame!"

"I do not see that it is. It would give me no particular pleasure to join your company, and I shall have that precious time to myself."

"Well, the dinner will be all the duller. My aunt will be as black as thunder. You know she wanted to marry Hugh, her second son, to Mary Dacre. You never met Hugh?"

"Why, I am not yet two months in Mrs Saville's service."

"What a very unvarnished way of putting it!" said Lumley, laughing.

"I never object to the truth," returned

Miss Desmond. "Why should I not *serve* Mrs Saville for the time being?"

"I am sure I don't know. Well, Hugh is a capital fellow, but awfully headstrong: so, after he was sent ashore last time, he went wandering about the Continent, and fell in love with a charming girl, or a girl he thought charming, without asking leave. Rather imprudent, eh?"

"It was more," said Hope, looking dreamily far away. "It was wrong. A good mother has a right to be consulted."

"Perhaps so; but if a fellow is very much in love he is apt to forget these things. Anyhow, Hugh has been chivied away from the maternal roof. It seems my uncle, Lord Everton, introduced Hugh to the fair one and her father, so he has been tabooed too; but he is a remarkably plucky old boy, so he came down here to plead Hugh's cause, and caught it pretty hard, I fancy."

"Yes, I saw him, and I imagine he had a trying time of it. Pray, do you—I mean your special family—talk of each other to every one in this candid fashion ? "

"I do ; and why should I not ? I say nothing that every one doesn't know and talk about."

"Poor Lord Everton ! " said Hope, with a laugh, as if she enjoyed the recollection. "He did look as if he were being led to execution when he was leaving the room and asked me to pray for him."

"Oh, he did, did he ? He's no end of fun."

"I can imagine he is. Good morning, Captain Lumley."

"Why, where the deuce— *Must* you go ? "

" I must. I do not know whether Mrs Saville may want me, and I have no business to wander about the grounds with you."

"Perhaps you may be at dinner, after all."

" It is not probable. If Lord Everton were to be of the party I might wish to intrude myself. As it is—good-bye for the present."

With a pleasant nod and smile, Miss Desmond turned into a path which led directly to the house, and left the gallant hussar lamenting.

" She is handsomer than I thought," he mused. " What eyes !—and such a smile ! She has rather taken to *me*, I can see that, but there is something unflatteringly self-possessed and frank about her. Treats me as if I were a mere boy. I must be very civil to the heiress. If my father thinks I am making any running there, I dare say he will pay some of my debts."

Lumley's wishes were fulfilled, for Mrs Saville, shortly before the dressing-bell rang, commanded Miss Desmond's presence at dinner. That young lady hesitated, and said with her usual good-humoured frankness, "You are always so good to me, that you may possibly ask me to dine as a civility, but I assure you I would prefer the evening to myself."

"You are quite mistaken. I wish you to dine with us to-day. Why, is of no consequence. I may not always ask you, but, when I do, be sure I mean it."

"Oh, very well. I am glad you have made matters clear."

It was a small party, and not very lively. Richard Saville was not an animated host. Mrs Saville was not talkative. The vicar was a pleasant, well-bred man, and with the help of Lumley, who was always ready to talk, kept the party from stagnating.

Lumley had brought with him, by his aunt's invitation, a young subaltern, the son of an acquaintance, who made the eighth and balanced the sexes. This youth fell to Hope Desmond's lot, much to his satisfaction, for she managed to make him talk, and talked to him easily and naturally, confessing her ignorance of hunting, shooting, fishing and sport of every kind, rather to his amazement. However, she atoned for her deficiencies by listening with much interest to his descriptions and explanations. At last he suggested giving her riding-lessons, at which she held up her hands in dismay. Miss Dacre interested her more than any one else. She had never been in the society of a great heiress, a prospective peeress in her own right. "What a tremendous position for a young girl!" thought Hope, with a curious sort of pity. The young girl was, notwithstanding, quite girlish, not pretty, but far from plain. She was very dark, with small, sparkling black eyes, curly black hair, and a high colour. She had a neat figure, and carried herself well, yet she lacked distinction.

"She might be a very pleasant companion," mused Hope, as she gazed at her while her cavalier was explaining the difference between a snaffle and a curb, "and considering her gifts, I am not surprised that Mrs Saville would have liked her for a daughter-in-law. How much, according to her estimate, her son appears to have thrown away!"

During the brief separation of the sexes

after dinner Miss Dacre naturally fell into Hope Desmond's care.

"How charming the conservatory looks!" she said. "Shall we walk round it?" Hope assented, not aware of the curiosity she excited in the future Baroness Castleton. That Mrs Saville should institute a companion was one source of astonishment; that any one so chosen should survive nearly two months and present a cheerful, self-possessed, composed aspect, was another. "And how nice she looks in that pretty, soft black grenadine and lace! How snowy white her throat and hands are! I suppose she is in mourning. Girls never want to be companions unless all their people die. Poor thing! I think I would rather be a housemaid; at least one might flirt with the footman; but a companion!—"

H

"I don't think I ever met you here before," she said, aloud.

"No; I am not quite two months with Mrs Saville."

"Poor Mrs Saville! she is looking so ill. They say she is rather a terrific woman. I always found her very nice."

"She is a strong woman, but there is a certain grandeur in her character."

"Yes, and I fancy one must be pretty strong to get on with her," said Miss Dacre, and she gave a knowing little nod to her companion. "Then she is so awfully put out about Hugh. You came after he had gone."

Hope bent her head as an affirmative.

"He was charming, quite charming—so different from Richard—though I like Richard too; but Hugh had a sort of rough good breeding, if you can understand such a thing; he was so generous

and bright and natural. I knew both
the brothers since I was quite a little
child, so I can sympathise with Mrs
Saville. To think of his having married
some designing woman abroad, twice his
age, I believe! isn't it horrible?" ran on
the talkative young lady.

"Horrible!" echoed Hope. "I trust
she is conscious of all he has sacrificed
for her."

"Not she," returned Miss Dacre, with
decision. "These sort of people haven't
an idea what family and position, and all
that, mean. Do you think Mrs Saville
would mind· if I plucked some of these
lovely waxen blossoms?"

"I am sure she would not; but you
know her much better than I do. Wait
a moment; I will get you the scissors."

"Pray," asked Miss Dacre, when she
returned, "are you Irish? You don't

mind my asking? Some people don't like the Irish: I delight in them. My father's great friend is an old general, a dear old thing—Sir Patrick Desmond is he any relation of yours?"

"I have heard of him, but if he is in any way connected with me, it is so distant that I cannot 'call cousins' with him."

"If he comes down to The Court while you are here, I will ask you to meet him. Then you are Irish? And I am sure you sing and play?"

"I play a little."

"That is delightful. You can play an accompaniment? I can't bear playing; and I want to try some duets with George Lumley to-night."

"I will do my best,' said Hope.

"Don't you think George Lumley very good-looking? He is very good style, too, and so like Lord Everton. I am rather glad he is at Hounslow. This place is too far, and yet too near, to be amusing," etc., etc. And she chattered on, till the gentlemen came to seek them in their fragrant retreat, when Miss Dacre ceased to bestow attention or words on Hope. They soon adjourned to the larger drawing - room, where the singers discovered that Miss Desmond had quite a genius for playing accompaniments, and time flew fast till the carriages were announced."

"Where in the world did you find that nice Miss Desmond, Mrs Saville ? " exclaimed Miss Dacre. "She is so quiet and well bred. Lots to say, too. Do bring her over to The Court. She could be of infinite use to me in playing accompaniments."

"Very likely ; but, you see, I engaged her to be of use to *me*."

"To be sure," laughed the thoughtless

girl. " How frightfully sharp you are ! "
And she blew her hostess a kiss as she
left the room.

" What a glorious night ! " said Lumley,
with a sigh of relief, sinking on an ottoman beside Hope. " Couldn't you manage
to come out for a stroll before saying
good-night finally ? "

Hope looked at him for a moment,
gravely, then a smile began in her eyes
and sparkled on " lip and cheek."

" Yes, it could be easily managed,
according to novel regulations," she said.
" I escort my kind patroness to her room,
receive her blessing, and return to my
own ; then I throw a mantilla over my
beautiful locks, steal down to the garden
door, which is, of course, left open, and,
guided by the perfume of a fine cigar,
join you in the moonlit shrubbery."

" Precisely," said Lumley, laughing.

" It's a lovely picture. I earnestly hope you will realise it."

"*Le jeu ne vaut pas la chandelle,*" she returned, rising and making him a slight curtsey. "A moonlight stroll is a harmless amusement under certain conditions, which do not exist at present for me." And she went away to bid goodnight to the vicaress and see that she was wrapped up. Then, meeting Mrs Saville on her way upstairs, she accompanied her to her bedroom, rang for her maid, and exchanged a few words with her until that functionary appeared.

"I am wofully tired," said Mrs Saville, throwing herself into a low chair. "Really, life is too wearisome in its disappointing sameness. If Richard will invite these stupid, chattering boys, I shall dine in my own room. Mary Dacre is sillier than she used to be, and Mr

Rawson writes that he cannot come down till the Sunday after next. We must begin *Froment Jeune* to - morrow, Miss Desmond, and get away as much as we can from the present."

"I shall be very pleased. It is considered one of Daudet's best, and I have never read it."

When Hope Desmond reached her own room she undressed rapidly and, putting out the candles, brushed her long hair by the moonlight, while she thought earnestly, "How disappointing of Mr Rawson! I hoped he would be here next Sunday; and I have so much to say to him. True, I can write; but a few spoken words face to face are worth a dozen letters. It will not be easy to get him to myself, but as my own especial friend I have a right to demand an interview. How weary that poor woman is!—and far from well. Poor

and nearly friendless as I am, I would
not change with her. No, no; I understand life better than she does, though
she has lived so much longer. How her
heart must ache when she thinks of her
son! Under all her hardness and pride
she yearns for the love she does not know
how to win. If she will only love me!"
Then she twisted up her hair, and, throwing herself on her knees, prayed long and
fervently, with tightly-clasped hands, while
tears streamed unheeded from the eyes
that less than an hour ago had smiled so
saucily on Captain Lumley.

"The two months have nearly expired,"
she mused, when, having risen, she leaned
against the window-frame and looked out
on the moonlit lawn. "But I am quite
sure she will not send me away. I do
not want to go among strangers again. It
is awful to have no home. But with

practice, with the effort to seem brave, courage comes."

Taking some relic sewn up in a little silk bag, and hung round her neck by a thin chain of Indian gold, she kissed it lovingly and lay down to rest.

For the next couple of days Mrs Saville instituted a severe headache, and shut herself up with Miss Desmond in her own special morning-room, leaving her son and his guest to entertain each other. The third day Hope went out for a short stroll, as Mrs Saville evidently did not want her company in a visit she went to pay at The Court.

She had not gone far when she was overtaken by George Lumley, who immediately began to condole with her on what he was pleased to term her "false imprisonment." She talked with him gaily enough, but always with what he chose to term " a tinge of indulgence " in her manner, and then turned homeward sooner than she would otherwise have done.

" I must bid you good-bye. I am going back to my quarters this evening," he said. " But I shall be at The Court next week. I do hope you'll come and help us in those duets. Miss Dacre has planned no end of practising."

" I shall be glad to help you if I may."

" How submissive you are."

" Would you, a soldier, suggest mutiny ? "

" Our duties are very different."

" Nevertheless, duty *is* duty."

" You must have an awfully dull time of it."

" I do not feel dull. Mrs Saville is a very intelligent woman, and, as we differ on every subject we have abundance of interesting conversation."

"I should think so. Do you ever convert her?"

"I am afraid not; but I may make a little impression; constant dropping, you know, effects something. I want to convert her to the belief that man does not live by bread alone."

"I see; that he wants the sugar-plums of true love. How tame and flat life is without them! I think I understand; that jolly old boy Rawson has put you here to be Hugh's advocate."

"By no means. He recommended me as a suitable person to act as reader and amanuensis to your aunt, and I hope to do him credit."

"Do you know you puzzle me immensely?"

"A little mental exercise will do you good."

"Mental exercise! you give my mind plenty to do. You are never out of my thoughts."

"Good-morning, Captain Lumley," said Miss Desmond, with great composure. "I shall go in by the side door." And she turned down a narrow path which led to a private entrance at the foot of the stair communicating with a wing which contained Mrs Saville's rooms.

Lumley stood for a moment uncertain what to do. He dared not follow her, and he was reluctant to confess himself checkmated. His generally placid face grew set and stormy.

"What an infernally provoking woman! She treats me as if I were a mere schoolboy, whom she could play with in safety. It is no longer play to me; it *shall* not

be play to her. I never was treated in
this way before; and there is an odd sort
of liking for me under it all. What
speaking eyes she has! I have seen
dozens of handsomer women, but there's
a sort of fascination about her. I will
not let her foil me." He walked rapidly
away to the lonely recesses of the wood,
more disturbed and resolute than he had
ever felt in his self-indulged life. All
his fancies had been so quickly and easily
gratified that they had scarcely time to
crystallise into activity; now he was
almost surprised at the vehemence of his
own anger and determination. "And if
I do succeed in awakening something of
passion in her, how will it end?" was a
question that passed through his brain.
"Time enough to think of that. At all
events, I am an only son, and the estates
are entailed."

The Sunday but one after this interview, Mr Rawson came down in time for
church. Mrs Saville chose to stay at
home. The service was short, for the
vicar did not think it necessary to give
a sermon every week. When it was over,
there was a gathering of neighbours and
greetings outside the porch.

"I wish you would come back to
luncheon, Miss Desmond," said Miss Dacre.
"You might, as Mrs Saville is not here.
Lord Everton came rather unexpectedly
last night, and I am sure you would like
him. He has been asking if you are still
alive."

"I am very sorry I cannot assure him
personally of my safety; but I cannot
absent myself in this unceremonious
manner. Then I have my friend Mr
Rawson here."

"What a nuisance! I am coming over

after luncheon to ask for assistance in getting up a concert to collect funds for a new school-house; so, till this afternoon, adieu." She stepped into her pony-carriage, attended by Richard Saville, and drove away.

"As we have plenty of time, I will take you by a little longer way back, Mr Rawson," said Hope.

"I place myself in your hands, my dear young lady." As they started, Lumley, who had stood aside till Miss Dacre drove off, joined them, and for a short way the conversation was chiefly between him and the family lawyer.

Lumley had been exceedingly nice and respectful whenever he had met Hope Desmond during the last week, consequently they had been the best of friends, and the captain flattered himself he was making prodigious strides. Arriving at a bend of the road where a turnstile admitted to a pathway leading across a field and into Mrs Saville's woods, Miss Desmond paused, and said "Good-morning" very decidedly.

"Mr Rawson is good enough to be my guardian, and I claim the right to bore him with my affairs whenever I can."

"I understand," said the gallant hussar, good-humouredly, and stopped with a bow.

"That stroke was well played," said Mr Rawson when they had got clear of the gate. "I want to say and to hear a good deal, and the youth is persevering."

"Is he so young?" asked Hope. "I thought him an amusing boy, but I begin to see he is older than I imagined."

"He will never see twenty-seven again. But to business. I am glad to see you

I

get on so well with Mrs Saville. I
thought you would."

"Yes, better than I expected. It was
terribly nervous work at first. Firm-
ness and courage are indispensable; the
slightest appearance of the white feather,
and she would almost unconsciously
crush you. It is not easy to impress
her gently and politely with a sense of
one's complete independence; but this
is essential. The tyrannical tendencies in
her have been tremendously developed
by circumstances and training; but I
really believe it is a relief to her to
find a companion who neither quarrels
nor cringes; she breathes a freer air,
her mind is more healthily exercised.
I never conceal an opinion, and I try
to be as true as possible, and to
defend my views as temperately as I
can. I also try to give her the im-

pression that she is on trial as well as myself."

"It is a dangerous game; but you may succeed. The day after to-morrow completes your two months. I suspect she would be sorry if you left. Tell me, have you had a chance of putting in a word for the poor prodigal?"

Hope shook her head. "It is too soon to attempt it," she said.

"Now sit down here on this fallen tree; for I have a long story to tell you."

CHAPTER VI

MISS DACRE was a very persevering young woman, nor was she restrained by any sensitive delicacy in pursuing her designs. Hitherto she had rather liked Mrs Saville in a surface fashion, flattering herself that she was a favourite with the stern little woman.

On this supposed favouritism she was always ready to presume. Hope Desmond and Mr Rawson were therefore somewhat appalled when the sounds of voices and approaching footsteps in the pleasure-ground, to which the windows of the smaller drawing-room opened, made themselves heard about tea-time, when Mrs

Saville had come in from a short stroll with her confidential adviser, and Hope had descended from her own room, where she had enjoyed a couple of hours' solitude. These sounds were followed by the appearance of Miss Dacre, Saville, Lumley and Lord Everton, accompanied by two or three dogs, at which Prince immediately barked defiance, scrambling up on his mistress's sofa for that purpose.

" So sorry you were not able to come to church this morning, dear Mrs Saville ! " said Miss Dacre, effusively, and with the unconcerned assurance of the class which does not hesitate to rush in where the sharper-sighted fear to tread ; "so we have all come over to inquire for you. You are looking quite pale. You see I have brought poor Lord Everton, who is so distressed at being expelled from this paradise. You really must make friends. He could not foresee that things would go wrong, and he *is* so sorry. Now, for my sake, dear Mrs Saville, you must forgive him, you are such near relations."

"Connections, you mean," corrected Mrs Saville, a bitter smile curling her lip. "If Lord Everton chooses to come, I can only admire his forgiving nature and accept the olive-branch."

"You are, as ever, just and generous," returned the impecunious peer, with a delightful bow and smile. "I am quite charmed with the vision of myself as a dove, which you kindly suggest."

Mrs Saville turned from him with undisguised contempt, and addressed herself to George Lumley.

"So you are staying at The Court? How does your regiment, or your troop, get on without your valuable assistance?"

"Disagreeable old cat!" thought Lumley,

while he said, "Oh, I ride over every other day, and the intermediate ones they stumble on as best they can without me."

"I thought you were going down to Herondyke?"

"Here's metal more attractive," said Lumley melodramatically, with a wave of his hand towards Miss Dacre, who was deep in conversation with Mr Rawson, on whom she was smiling with her habitual belief in her own power to fascinate all male creatures.

"Metal! Yes, I dare say. I sometimes wonder if you are as foolish as you seem, George."

"Oh, a good deal more so," said the handsome hussar, showing his white teeth in a pleasant smile. "You know I haven't many ideas."

"Yet I daresay you would be less easily taken in than men who have," scornfully.

" Very probably, my dear aunt."

" What is the matter with you ? " asked Miss Dacre, in a low tone, drawing a chair to the tea-table, where Hope Desmond presided. " You look pale and ill, and as if you had been crying. Pray forgive me," she added, seeing the quick colour rise in her victim's cheek, " but I knew quite well you could not stand Mrs Saville for long," in a low tone.

"Oh, yes, I can," said Hope, smiling a brave defiance. "Don't you think I am likely to have worries and bad news apart from poor Mrs Saville ? "

" Well, I suppose so ; but it did not occur to me. She is not popular, you know, though I always get on with her. I am going to play a bold stroke just now ; it will astonish you all. 'Nothing venture nothing have,' you know."

" 'Jockey of Norfolk, be not too bold,' "

quoted Miss Desmond, with a somewhat tremulous smile.

" She has been crying—I am certain she has ; though she is braving it out. At any rate, she is going to stick to Mrs Saville. I wonder what *she* is saying to George Lumley ? Nothing amiable, I am sure."

Here Lord Everton, who had been speaking to Saville, and of whom the mistress of the house had not taken the slightest notice, approached and begged for a cup of tea.

" It is a beverage of which I am extremely fond," he said, " and I think a decided liking for tea ought to be a patent of respectability to any man. Ah," he added, on taking the cup from her hands, " you never put up one little prayer for me on that trying occasion, you remember ? "

"I did not know what to pray for."

"Oh, for my deliverance generally; so, instead, I was delivered into the hands of the tormentor."

"I am glad to see you have completely recovered."

"The shield of a good conscience, the sword of an innocent spirit brought me through the ordeal."

"Then you did not want my prayers."

"Yet I deserved them."

"Indeed! Why?"

"I shall explain my claims one day, in the silent recesses of some tangled wood, say in the jungle between this mansion and the vicarage." And the lively old gentleman laughed with almost boyish glee at Hope's rather puzzled expression.

"You have been a good deal on the

Continent, I believe, Miss Desmond ? " he resumed.

"I have travelled occasionally in my aunt's lifetime."

"Ah ! and enjoyed it, I dare say ? "

"Yes ; but I also enjoy returning to England."

"Indeed ! Well, I do not. The moment I set foot on my native shore, I cease to be a free man ; invisible detectives put me in social irons ; cruel warders imprison me within adamantine barriers, where I am obliged to eat and drink and speak and have my being according to rigid rules. I must give my money for what satisfieth not, and go to the funereal hostelries frequented by my peers. I must don evening-dress, and wear unlimited purple and fine linen. Then my exasperating relatives will pester me with invitations, because they think they must not neglect 'that poor old beggar Everton. Now, on the other side of the Channel my only habitation is an airy bedroom, *au quatrième,* outside which a whole world of cafés and restaurants are 'before me where to choose' my breakfast and dinner, where I meet pleasant, intelligent people of every shade of opinion, with whom I can converse freely in happy ignorance of their names and condition, as they are of mine; and occasionally I stumble on old acquaintances who enjoy life in my own fashion, cheerfully accepting the contemptuous treatment of Dame Fortune, who in emptying our pockets also relieved us of tiresome responsibilities. It is wonderful the clearness of judgment and general enlightenment of those who are not weighed down by this world's goods."

"I dare say you are right, Lord Everton.

Still, a few of them are advantageous; though I do not see that money can purchase any essential of life."

"That depends very much on what you consider essentials."

"That is true— But Miss Dacre is going to make a speech," for that young lady had said, in an audible tone, "I am going to tell you a story."

"I know," whispered Lord Everton. "If her pockets had always been empty, she would have known better how to hold her tongue."

"This story came to me in a letter from the wife of a cousin of mine, whose cousin was eye-witness of the adventure," Miss Dacre was saying, as she posed herself on an ottoman and every one turned towards her. "Scene: a dark, stormy night, a distant sea, one of Her Majesty's big ships tossing about on the waves, which make

nothing of her bigness. Young sailor,
doing something incomprehensible with a
rope or ropes, loses hold or balance and
drops into the black depths of the raging
waters. Captain orders boat to be lowered.
'He'll be gone before you can reach him,'
they say. 'He cannot swim,' cries another
officer, throwing off his shoes or boots (I
do not know which they wear on board
ship) while he spoke, and springing over
the side at a bound.

" 'This is suicide,' exclaimed the captain.
The young officer is a huge favourite with
the crew, the crew work with a will, the
boat is lowered away, a life-boat, probably ;
they surmount the waves and slide into
the watery hollows ; they come up with
the gallant lieutenant, who is supporting
the senseless sailor and nearly exhausted
himself ; they drag them into the boat ;
they regain the ship, the men crowd round

the—whatever you call it where they get on board, their cheers ring above the roar of the storm, the rescued and rescuer are safe ! "

" Most dramatic," said Lord Everton.

" Worthy of Brandram," added George Lumley.

" I don't exactly see—" began Richard Saville.

" No, of course you do not : there is nothing to see exactly," interrupted Miss Dacre, quickly.

" I have heard the tale before. The only difference is that the weather was not quite so stormy as you—your correspondent, I mean, represents it," said Mr Rawson, playing with his double glasses.

" It was really much worse than I represent," exclaimed Miss Dacre, with an air of profound conviction. " Now, does no one want to know the name of my hero ?"

There was a moment's pause. Mrs Saville sat silent in her arm-chair, stroking with a steady hand the silky head of her little dog, a half-smile curling her lip. Lumley's laughing eyes sought Miss Desmond's, but she was sheltered behind a massive urn which always appeared at tea-time. Only Lord Everton rose to the occasion.

"I am dying of curiosity, my dear Miss Dacre," he said, languidly.

"Name! name!" cried Lumley.

"Hugh Saville!" said Miss Dacre, rising and assuming an attitude.

"I thought so," said Richard.

"Just like him!" cried Lumley, cordially.

"Give me your arm, Mr Rawson. I have letters to show you in my study. I avoided church because I did not think prayers or sermon would improve my headache. I did not bargain for being obliged to sit out a dramatic recital," said Mrs Saville, dryly; then added to the company, "You will excuse me, I do not feel equal to general conversation." Holding Prince under her left arm, she touched Mr Rawson's with the finger-tips of her right hand, and walked with much dignity through the door which Lord Everton, with a sad and solemn expression of countenance, held open.

As soon as she had passed, he closed it gently, and, advancing a step or two, glanced from one to the other with so comic a look of dismay that both Lumley and Saville laughed.

"Courage such as yours, my dear Miss Dacre, deserved success; and yet it has not been successful," he said, with an air

K

of deep sympathy, to the fair narrator, and sat down on the ottoman beside which she stood.

"I never saw any one like Mrs Saville —never!" cried Miss Dacre, growing red with disappointment and mortification. "I really hoped that such a story of bravery and humanity would have done something towards softening her heart, and I flatter myself I did it pretty well."

"If you had asked my advice," said Richard Saville, "I could have told you it would be simple waste of breath."

"But," exclaimed Miss Dacre, with a sound of tears in her voice, "Mrs Saville always used to mind what I said, and— and seemed so fond of me. I was rather proud of it, she likes so few people."

"I am afraid there is some difference between past and present," said Lumley, pushing a chair forward. "Come, Miss

Dacre, you have done your best, and your best is very good. Now take a cup of tea, and pardon my aunt her scant courtesy. I am going to write to Hugh, and I'll tell him of your championship."

"You ought," said Miss Desmond, who had not spoken before, but whose voice showed she had not been unmoved. "Very few can count on such courageous advocacy of the absent and of a losing cause."

"You are very kind to say so. Yes, I will have a cup of tea. My mouth feels parched."

"No wonder!" cried Lord Everton. " I am sure my tongue would have cleaved to the roof of mine, had I dared to utter such words to the Lion of Inglewood. Excuse me, my dear Richard."

"Do not mention it, my dear uncle."

"I wish you would come out and take a

little walk with me, Miss Desmond," said
Miss Dacre. "I feel frightfully upset."

"I should like to do so very much, but
Mrs Saville may want me to write for
her, or something, and I do not like to
be out of the way"

"Heavens! what penal servitude!" cried
Miss Dacre.

"You must not say so. I agree to per-
form certain duties, and it would not be
honest to run away from them."

"Why do you always take her part?"
and Miss Dacre made an impatient grimace.
Then, addressing the gentlemen, "I dare
say you are all dying to smoke, which Mrs
Saville will not permit in this part of the
house. Just go and have your cigars and
cigarettes outside, or walk back to The
Court, and I can follow by myself. Then I
can have a quiet talk with Miss Desmond."

"Very well," said Lumley, rising, "I

will escort my uncle to The Court, and return for you." Miss Dacre gave him a nod
and smile, and the gentlemen left them.

The young heiress was, as she said, much
upset, and, besides this, she had felt for
some time what she herself would have
termed an "aching void" for want of a
confidante. A confidante had always been
a necessity to her, as it generally is to
persons much taken up with themselves.
Her last devoted friend, the depositary
of her secret troubles, projects and love-
affairs, had lately married a brutal husband,
who had taught his bride to laugh at Mary
Dacre's storms in a teacup and twopenny-
halfpenny tragedies; so her heart was
empty, swept and garnished, and ready for
the occupation of another "faithful friend
and counsellor," when fate threw Hope
Desmond in her way. In Miss Dacre's
estimation, she was eminently fitted to fill

the vacant post; there was just the difference of station between them which would
make the confidences of the future Baroness
Castleton flattering to their recipient, to
whom also her friendship might be useful.
There was a short pause. Miss Desmond's
eyes looked dreamy, as if she were gazing
in spirit at some distant scene, and not
as if she were quivering with impatience
for the revelations about to be made
to her.

The silence was broken suddenly by a
somewhat unconnected exclamation from
Miss Dacre : " He is certainly very nice-
looking."

" Who ? Lord Everton ? " asked Hope.

" Lord Everton ! Nonsense ! He might
have been forty years ago. I mean
Captain Lumley. There is something
knightly in his look and bearing : one
could imagine him going down into the

lion's pit for one's glove, and that sort of thing."

"I do not think I could," smiling. "I do not fancy Captain Lumley or any other logical modern young man doing anything of the kind. He might, if extra chivalrous, bring you a dozen new pairs from Jouvin's to replace the one you had dropped."

" Ah, my dear Miss Desmond, I fear you are not imaginative. .Or perhaps you have only known prosaic men."

"I have only known very few of any kind."

"And I have had such a wide experience!" said Miss Dacre, with a sigh. " You can see I am no beauty ; yet I have the fatal gift of fascination in an extraordinary degree. Yes, really, it is quite curious. Of course ill-natured people say it is *les beaux yeux de ma cassette ;* but no one who is not very dull can be

deceived in these things." Another sigh.
" I feel in something of a difficult position
just now, and I have no friend near with
whom to take counsel.   Now, dear Miss
Desmond, I feel attracted to you.   I am
certain you could be a faithful friend,
and silent as the grave."

" I should be very happy to be of any
use to you," said Hope, seeing she paused
for a reply.

" I knew you would.   I am so tired
of feeding on my own heart !   I want a
friend.   Now, I dare say you are surprised to see how earnestly I advocate
Hugh Saville's cause.   Ah, there is a
little tragic story which will colour my
whole life."

" Indeed ! "   with awakening interest.
" I trust your life will be free from all
tragic ingredients."

" Ah, no ; that it cannot be.   You

must know that I saw a great deal of
Richard and Hugh Saville when I was
a little girl; my father worried a great
deal about politics, and I used to live at
The Court all the summer, that he might
see me sometimes (my mother died when
I was a baby, you know). Well, as soon
as I left off playing with dolls and began
to feel, I was in love with Hugh; and
he was very fond of me. Then he went to
sea, and we did not meet for years, until
after I had been presented, and had refused
half a dozen men. I shall never forget
our first meeting when he returned from
—oh, I don't know where. He was so
pleased to see me ; but soon, very soon, I
saw that he who was the light of my eyes
was the one man of all I had met who
resisted the attraction I generally exercise."
Here she paused in her voluble utterance
and pressed her handkerchief to her eyes.

Hope was so amazed at these unexpected revelations that the bright colour
rose in her cheek—it seemed to her
delicate nature almost indecent thus to
lay bare one's secret experiences to a
stranger—and a look of embarrassment
made her drop her eyes; but these
symptoms were lost on her companion,
who thoroughly enjoyed holding forth
on the delightful topic of self and
exhibiting her own fine points.

" That must have been very trying,"
said Hope, feeling she ought to say
something.

" Awful, my dear Miss Desmond. By-
the-bye, may I call you Hope? It is a
good omen, your name."

" Certainly, Miss Dacre."

" Well, my dear Hope, I nearly went
mad ; but it is curious that I never looked
better. I flirted wildly with every one ;

still, of course, Hugh knew quite well
that I was desperately in love with him."

"Did he? How very trying! Perhaps he did not."

"Oh, yes, he did; and of course I did
all sorts of wild things to show I did
not care."

"Yes, I understand."

"Then I had that disturbance with my
father about poor Lord Balmuir. I behaved rather badly. I did intend to
marry him, but I couldn't! And so we
went abroad; and I felt better. But it
was an awful blow when I found that
Hugh was absolutely married! Just think
of it!—and to a mere adventuress, a nobody!—such an ambitious man! He will
get sick of her, you may be quite sure."

"Why?" asked Hope, looking earnestly
at her. "Is he very changeable?"

"No, not at all; he is as steady as a

rock, and very proud. But most men tire of their wives, especially when they have brought them no advantages. I never thought Hugh Saville could fall in love and forget himself. Now, when I saw George Lumley, his likeness to his cousin made my heart beat. I soon saw that he was a good deal struck with me, and I believe I could love him passionately if --if memory was not so importunate. He is very charming; and why should I not grow young again? for one does feel awfully old when one has no love-affair on. Don't you think George Lumley is —very much taken with me? "

"I suppose that sort of attraction is more perceptible to its object than to any one else," returned Hope Desmond, hesitatingly. She had grown pale and grave, while Miss Dacre rattled on:

"Then, you see, when I heard about

Hugh saving that man's life, I thought
I might make use of the story to wake
up Mrs Saville's good feelings. It would
be rather an heroic proceeding if I were
to reconcile the mother, son and wife.
George Lumley said I was splendidly
generous."

"What! did he, too, know all about
Hugh—I mean Mr Saville?" cried Hope,
more and more disturbed.

"Oh, yes; we have quite interesting
talks about him. I tell him confidentially
how fond I was of Hugh, and then, of
course, he wishes he was in Hugh's place:
so we get on very well. He is always
coming over to The Court, except when
he goes away for a few days' shooting.
I am not quite sure my father likes it.
You have never met Lord Castleton? He
is very nice—rather old-fashioned, and
high Tory. Lord Everton was a great

friend of his in early days. Now, my
dear Hope, you know my heart-history ;
and you will notice Captain Lumley's
manner. You know the Lumley estates
are rather encumbered, and I dare say he
feels shy of approaching me—poor fellow !
but, if I like him (and I do), that is of
no consequence."

" I am always interested in what you
like to tell me, Miss Dacre," said Hope,
with some hesitation, as if choosing her
words, "but I am not very observant,
and some older and wiser person would
be more deserving of your confidence
than I am."

" Nonsense ! I could not tell all these
things to a stiff old frump ! Now, mind
you ask Mrs Saville if you may come
and practise every morning for the concert. I intended to ask her, but my
anxiety about Hugh quite put it out of

my head. That is always my way I never think of myself." Hope was too bewildered with her energetic rapidity to reply, so Miss Dacre went on: "She has really no feeling at all. She is fearfully hard. I am afraid she will never forgive Hugh. But I will do all I can."

"If you will take my advice, Miss Dacre," said Hope, earnestly, "you will leave the matter alone. The less Mrs Saville hears of her son for the present, the better. Attempts to force him on her notice only hardens her."

"Well, perhaps so; but you must back me up whenever you can."

"Trust me, I will."

"Now, I had better go home. I dare say Captain Lumley is waiting for me on the way. I am so glad that you made me open my heart to you. It is such a comfort to have some one to speak to."

"Thank you," returned Hope.

"So good-bye. You are looking quite pale and ill. Be sure you ask Mrs Saville about the concert." And Miss Dacre departed through the open window.

Hope threw herself on the sofa as soon as she was gone, and sat there lost in thought, her elbow on the cushion, her head on her hand, unconscious of the large tears which, after hanging on her long lashes, rolled slowly down her cheeks. What unhappiness and con-fusion Hugh Saville's headstrong dis-obedience had created!—and for what? Perhaps only for a temporary whim; perhaps only to regret it, as Miss Dacre said. The thought of these things depressed .her. Some incident in her own life perhaps made her more keenly alive to the trouble in Mrs Saville's;

for Hope Desmond was an exceedingly
attractive girl, graceful, gentle, with
flashes of humour and fire, suggesting
delightful possibilities. The day had
been trying, for her good friend Mr
Rawson had not brought too flourishing an account of her affairs, and she
did not enjoy the idea of being *demoiselle de compagnie* all her life. At
this stage of her reflections a shadow
fell across her, and, looking up, she saw
George Lumley contemplating her with
much interest. She was always pleased
to see his bright, good-looking face,
and, smiling on him kindly, said,
"You have missed Miss Dacre. She
has just gone."

"Are you all right, Miss Desmond?"
he asked, with much interest, and
drawing a step nearer.

"Yes, of course," she returned; then,

L

becoming suddenly aware that her face was wet with tears, she blushed vividly and put up her handkerchief to remove them.

"The terrible effect of a private interview with one's legal adviser," she said, with a brave attempt to laugh.

"He must have brought you bad news, I fear." And Lumley sat down beside her. "Old Rawson——" He paused.

"Is one of the best and kindest of friends," put in Hope. "Now, I must go away. I should have been in my room oefore this, only Miss Dacre chose to stay and talk about family affairs. If you follow you will soon overtake her; she has taken the vicarage path."

"Why, you don't suppose I want to overtake her?"

"She expects you."

"Well, she may do so. She has

nearly talked me to death once to-day. I am not going to run the same risk again."

Hope looked at him with a very puzzled expression, then a smile parted her lips.

"I think you are all very curious people here," she said. "There are small signs of English reserve about you. But I don't want to hear any more confidences : so I shall leave you."

"This is too bad !—when I thought I should have a minute's talk with you in peace ! Did you ever know anything so idiotic as Miss Dacre's dramatic attempt ? "

"I thought you pronounced it 'splen-didly generous.'"

"Well, so it was, considering how mad she was about Hugh herself a couple of years ago. It was a match that would have suited my aunt down to the ground but he would never hear of it. Are you really going? Well, it is too bad of you! I hope you will not go over to this practising to-morrow? I am on duty, and have to return to quarters to-night."

"What I can or cannot do depends on Mrs Saville. Good-bye for the present." She gave him her hand for a moment, and was gone.

With an air of extreme annoyance, Captain Lumley lit a cigar, and, stepping through one of the open windows, followed the path taken by Miss Dacre.

The dinner at Inglefield was very tranquil that evening. Mrs Saville, her son, Hope Desmond and Mr Rawson made up the whole party. Mrs Saville looked ill; there were deep shadows under her eyes, and her face seemed smaller than usual;

but she was unusually talkative and gracious.

She discussed politics with her guest, and occasionally directed her remarks to Hope. Mr Saville contributed some rather original observations, and all things went smoothly. On leaving the table she said to Rawson, "I must leave you to Miss Desmond's care this evening, for I have a very bad headache; but I shall see you in the morning."

After a little conversation, Mr Saville went to look for some sketches he had taken of the Lincolnshire churches, and in his absence Mr Rawson said, "Mrs Saville is most friendly. She particularly wishes you to remain; she says you know when to be silent and when to speak; so I think things promise well. Go on as you have begun. She talks of going on the Continent in a month or two. You are, I imagine, firmly fixed in her good graces. This is having half your work done."

" God grant it ! " said Hope, with heart-felt earnestness ; and soon after they separated for the night.

CHAPTER VII

"I THINK, Miss Desmond, I shall go abroad next week," said Mrs Saville, breaking silence one dull, drizzling, depressing November day, when they were sitting by the fire in the smaller of the two drawing-rooms. Mrs Saville had been in deep thought, and Hope diligently making a long strip of lace which usually occupied her when *tête-à-tête* with her patroness and not reading aloud.

"Do you wish me to accompany you?"

"Yes, of course. You are very ready to leave me."

"No, indeed, Mrs Saville; I should be sorry to do so; but I wish you to feel quite free. The secret of comfort in such a relationship as ours is that we are not bound to each other."

There was another pause.

"Very likely," resumed Mrs Saville, as if she had been reflecting. "However, I do not wish to part company as yet. I must say you are one of the few young women—indeed, young or old—who have any common sense, though your ideas on some points are by no means sound."

"What are my chief errors?" asked Hope, with the pleasant fearlessness which was one of her chief attractions to the imperious little plutocrat.

"You are a sentimentalist in some directions, and you do not recognise the true value of money. The first is weakness; the second, wilful blindness."

"I dare say I am weak," returned Hope, laying down her work and speaking thoughtfully; "but do you know, Mrs Saville, I think I have a truer estimate of the value of money than yourself?"

"How do you make that out?" Mrs Saville spoke with some degree of interest.

"I know that a certain amount is necessary, that real poverty is degrading, that every right-minded individual will strive and toil for a sufficiency enough to secure independence and respectability; but, after that, what can money buy? Not health, nor a sense of enjoyment, nor intelligence, nor the perception of beauty, nor that crown of life, love. Very moderate means will permit of fullest pleasure in all these, but they must be all the free gift of nature: gold cannot buy them."

"And with them all," returned Mrs

Saville, "you can never lift your head above the obscurity of a mean position, if you only possess moderate means."

"That does not seem a hardship to me. It is true I never knew what ambition meant, and therefore I am no fair judge of what is essential to an ambitious spirit; but men have attained to great power and yet had but little money."

"Not often — not often; while to women, with their more limited sphere, money is still more essential. If every one was as philosophic as yourself, where should we be? Where would civilisation, inventions, improvement, employment, be, if men did not haste to become rich?"

"But I do not object to people becoming rich, and I acknowledge that men who amass large fortunes are often

benefactors to their fellows. I only urge
that great wealth is not essential to
individual happiness, and that men who
increase knowledge and social improvement, who invent and explore, are benefactors equally with those who make
the money which pays for it all."

"We are like the two knights who
fought over the colour of the shield,
Miss Desmond. You must grant that
if wealth cannot buy health it can at
least mitigate suffering; and it certainly
can buy esteem, if it cannot buy love.
As to love, who feels it except the
young and the imaginative? It is but
another form of selfishness; some quality
in another gratifies you or flatters you,
and you think that person essential to
your existence."

"There is something more in it than
that," said Hope, gently; "you *must*

know that. Did you never love any one
yourself ? "

" Yes ; at least I thought I did, and
small thanks I had for it. But I am not
sure that my reason is not too strong for
my affections."

" I think," said Hope, slowly, "that
you could love very much." She stopped,
and grew a little paler than usual. "Pardon me if I take a liberty in speaking
my opinion."

" No ; go on, you amuse me."   •

" We scarcely know what gifts we possess till circumstances call them out, and
yours may not have drawn out your
faculties in that direction. But I am
quite sure the remarkable strength of
your nature would make your love strong
too."

" Really, Miss Desmond, you are a
profound student of human nature. Un-

fortunately for the development of my affections, I am not what is called a lovable person."

"No," said Hope, quietly, "not what a surface observer would call lovable; you are too contemptuous of weakness, which you cannot understand; but if steadiness of purpose, a sense of justice, honour and loyalty, are worthy of love, you ought to be loved. When I came to you, my first inclination was to fear you, and I determined not to yield to it, or, if I found it insurmountable, to leave you. You cannot support the companionship of a spirit inferior to your own."

"And you consider yours equal to mine?" asked Mrs Saville, with a slight smile.

"I do," returned Hope, steadily. "You are my superior in knowledge, in experience, in ability, in strength of will; but my opinions, my individuality, are my own; I will never yield them to the mere authority of any creature, even to one I respect as I do you. If, in speaking as I think, I offend, we are not bound to live together a moment longer than is agreeable. I may love you one day; I will never allow myself to fear you."

"You are rather a curious girl. I do not wish people to fear me. Why should they?"

"I do not suppose you do; but you have a dominant will, which wealth gives you the power to exercise, and it colours your manner."

"I have always been well served."

"No doubt."

"Well, Miss Desmond, you have interested me a good deal, and, as you say, whenever I grow too tyrannical, or you grow too fearless, we can part company.

At any rate, you are more of a rational being than most young women. Now, as to my plans for this winter. I cannot stand being worried by the people I know in London, and my relations; so I propose going to Dresden, a town where one meets few English. I have had enough of my compatriots for the present. I shall come to Paris in the spring; and after—oh, that is too remote to think of. I had a letter this morning from Mary Dacre. She is staying in Yorkshire, at some wild country house, where she hunts and shoots in modern-young-lady fashion. She threatens to return here with her obedient father on the 17th, and that idiot George Lumley in her train. Lady Olivia writes that the preference dear Mary Dacre shows with such girlish simplicity for dear George is quite touching. Of course the Lumleys are enchanted at the possibility of such a marriage. I wonder does it ever occur to them to count up the number of aspirants Miss Dacre has encouraged and thrown over? I do not myself quite understand why George Lumley hung about here so much. I fancy he was rather laughing at the future Baroness Castleton ; and he is too much a Saville to do what he doesn't like, even for a wealthy marriage."

" I must say, Mrs Saville, that seems to me erring in the right direction."

" I suppose it does, to *you*. To me it seems weak self - indulgence, when you consider the position George Lumley is born to, and which he is bound to keep up."

" What a terrible birthright ! " returned Hope Desmond, laughing, as she resumed her lace-work, and, tea coming in at that moment, the conversation was interrupted.

Hope had been for four months Mrs Saville's constant companion, and, having got over the first almost overpowering inclination to fly from her awful presence, every day added to the steadiness of her nerve, and to her influence with her wealthy patroness. She, too, rejoiced in Miss Dacre's departure for more brilliant fields of conquest, as her constant demands on her new confidante's time and sympathies were rather exhausting. The village concert had been a great success, but the practisings which led up to it had been an equally great trial. Moreover, Captain Lumley's manners had caused her much annoyance. Preoccupied feeling had at first blinded her as to the true meaning of his attentions and efforts to escort her to and from The Court and

M

Inglefield House ; while the self-confident hussar was enraged, piqued, and above all fascinated, by the friendly, kindly unconsciousness of his aunt's attractive companion. He had never met anything like it before, and gradually prudence, worldliness, every consideration, became merged in an all-devouring desire to conquer the smiling indifference which baffled him, and to revenge the endless slights he thought he had received. At last he had torn himself away, hoping to renew the attack with fresh effect on his return. Meanwhile, he masked his batteries under a very overt flirtation with Miss Dacre.

Before starting for the Continent, Hope had leave of absence for two or three days, which she spent with her friend Miss Rawson. These were a refreshment to her spirit, and after much confidential talk and some necessary shopping she returned to her post.

The welcome accorded her by the self-contained mistress of Inglefield was warmer than she anticipated. Mrs Saville had missed her pleasant companionship. Her presence soothed and satisfied the imperious woman. The sincere respect she evinced was so thoroughly a free-will offering that it was more flattering to Mrs Saville's *amour propre* than the most elegantly-turned compliments from a luminary of fashion.

"You will go on and prosper, I have no doubt," were Mr Rawson's parting words, the day before the intending travellers started, when he had come to Inglefield on business.

"So far all goes fairly. If I can win Mrs Saville's confidence so completely

that she voluntarily mentions her offending son, I shall think I have done
well."

"It will be a long experiment, I fear;
but you have twelve months before
you."

"Yes; and who knows what a day
may bring forth?"

Twenty - four hours later saw Mrs
Saville and her companion dining at
Meurice's. In the former's youth this
hotel had been the favourite quarters of
the well-to-do English in Paris, and she
never left it. Hope Desmond had often
been in Paris before, but generally in
cheap *pensions* or very loftily-placed and
diminutive apartments; and her present
luxurious surroundings did not please
her as much as they saddened by the
memories and contrasts they evoked.

After a few days' rest, Mrs Saville set

out for Germany, and in the quiet routine
of their comfortable life there the current
of this "ower true tale" seemed to
stagnate.

CHAPTER VIII

Back in bright Paris, now decked in her garden-party dress of chestnut-blossoms, lilacs and laburnums, some six or seven months afterwards.

Mrs Saville had spent a very tranquil winter. She had rarely been free from irritation for so long a period.

For a week or two at Christmas she had been a good deal tried by a visit from her son, who, to her surprise, brought his cousin George Lumley with him. That over, she settled down again to her books, her fancy-work, of which she was rather proud, her game of whist with some old Grafs and Barons attached to the little court, some of whom had dabbled in diplomacy and even spent a few years in London, and frequent visits to the opera, for almost her only real pleasure was music.

If, six months before, Mrs Saville had missed her companion when she was absent for a couple of days, the idea of parting with her now would have struck her with dismay. She had softened gradually but considerably — so gradually that Hope Desmond had to look back and recall her first impressions to measure the change.

The weather was fine, the sky blue, and sunshine beautified all things. It seemed impossible not to partake of the general exhilaration which pervaded the atmosphere. Yet Mrs Saville's expression, if less hard, was infinitely sadder than formerly, and, though Miss Desmond's eyes were calm, and her air composed, there were shadows beneath the former and a somewhat worn look in her expressive face. She was thinner, too, as if she had borne some mental strain.

It was afternoon, and the Champs-Elysées were crowded with streams of equipages pouring out to the Bois. Stemming this current, Mrs Saville and Hope returned from their earlier drive, and on arriving at the hotel found another open carriage drawn up at the entrance, from which a gorgeously-dressed lady was leaning while she spoke to the porter. He made a gesture towards the new arrival, whereupon the lady looked round and displayed the well-known features of Miss Dacre.

"How fortunate!" she cried. "Here, open the door; let me out!" And she sprang upon the ground.

"My dear Mrs Saville, I only just heard by the merest accident that you were in Paris. We have been at Pau for two months, and are on our way home."

"Oh, indeed," returned Mrs Saville rather dryly, as she descended very deliberately and submitted to be kissed by her young friend. "I am sorry for your poor father. Why could you not let him rest in peace among his turnips and mangel-wurzels?"

"Why, I must think of myself sometimes, you know. How do you do, Hope? I am so glad to see you! I can't say you are looking very flourishing. I suppose you are coming in, so I can pay you a nice visit, though I have a hundred and one things to do. I suppose you have your old rooms, Mrs Saville. We are at the 'Bristol.' I wonder you stay here, it is so slow."

"Quite fast enough for me; but come upstairs."

"She is as cross as ever," whispered Miss Dacre to Hope as they ascended to Mrs Saville's apartments. "I don't wonder at your looking worn - out." Hope laughed and shook her head.

"You are comfortable enough here, I must say," resumed Miss Dacre, looking round the handsomely - furnished room, which was sweet with flowers and flooded with soft light, the strong sunshine filtering through the outer blinds.

"Well, dear Mrs Saville, and how are you after burying yourself alive in Germany all the winter? It is such a queer place to go to."

"*I* like Germany, and I am remarkably well."

"Well, you don't look so. We had a wild time at Herondyke. I was there for nearly a month. Lady Olivia is quite too good-natured. Then she and the girls came over to Castleton, but your son persuaded George Lumley to go with him to Dresden. A great mistake! Captain Lumley was quite cross when he returned—said it was a God-forgotten hole! I met Mr Vignolles at Pau," etc., etc. And Miss Dacre turned on a rapid flow of gossip. As soon as she made a pause for breath, Mrs Saville said wearily,—

"Miss Desmond, the tea is ready. Give me a cup."

"By all means. The Parisians have improved immensely, but they have not arrived at the height of good afternoon tea yet."

Silence on the part of Mrs Saville, while Miss Dacre sipped her tea.

"When do you come back to London. Mrs Saville ?"

"Not this year. I may go to Ingle-field in the autumn."

"I suppose you know Richard is bring-ing out a work on *The Romans in Lincolnshire*, illustrated, with notes and appendices *ad lib.?* It will cost a small fortune, they say."

'They? Who say?"

"Oh, the literary world. I am think-ing of publishing extracts from the Archives of Castleton Forest. There are lots of old deeds and letters in the muni-ment-room, especially about the Long Parliament times. One must really write something now."

"Indeed! Can't you compile a time-table of the trains between Castleton, Upton and London, copying Bradshaw freely? It would answer all purposes, and give you very little trouble."

"Dear Mrs Saville, what an idea!

Now, I want you to do me a favour.
Let Miss Desmond come with me to the
Opéra Comique this evening. They give
'Le petit Duc.' My father has insti-
tuted a headache, and I rather want a
chaperon. It will not be very late."

"Miss Desmond is perfectly free to
do as she likes."

"If you can find any other chaperon,
I am quite ready to stay at home," said
Hope, smiling.

"Now, do not be disagreeable. I
want you to come with me."

Hope did not answer, and after some
further *pour-parlers* it was arranged that
Miss Dacre should call for her favourite
confidante that evening *en route* for the
theatre.

"I have a hundred and one things to
say to you," whispered Miss Dacre when
Hope Desmond escorted her to the stair

after she had taken leave of Mrs Saville.
"The same mysterious fate still dogs me.
I do not know what spell binds George
Lumley to silence. Poor fellow! I am so
sorry for him! I rather imagined he
thought I was going to Dresden last
winter, heaven only knows why! You
will be ready at seven-thirty, will you
not?"

"Yes, certainly."

When Hope returned to Mrs Saville
she found that lady's maid removing her
out-door garb and arranging her mistress
on the sofa as if for a siesta.

"I would have saved you from this
infliction if I could," she said, presently,
when Hope thought she was going to
sleep, "but *politesse*, as well as *noblesse*,
oblige! Mary Dacre was always foolish;
she is now absolutely idiotic. I am not
surprised that Hugh had no patience

with her; Hugh was always instinctive. He is like me in many things."

Hope listened with nervous attention, growing alternately red and white. Never before had Mrs Saville named her offending son, and Hope feared to utter a word that might offend or divert the current of her thoughts.

" I am always doomed to disappointment," she went on, as if speaking out her thoughts. "There is Richard; he will be a dilettante and a nobody all the days of his life. I never wasted any anticipations on *him*. But Hugh might be anything—a statesman, a leader of men. I would have done anything to push his fortunes. All my hopes, all my ambitions, centred in him; and you know—you must have heard— how he repaid me."

"Yes, I have heard," returned Hope,

in such tremulous accents that Mrs Saville looked up, as if surprised and touched by her keen sympathy. "It seems very cruel."

"*Seems!* It *is*. To be forgotten, thrown over, for the sake of a pretty face, a whim of passion, after years of devotion! It is intolerable; it is not to be forgiven. An unsuitable wife is a millstone round a man's neck that will drag him to perdition; but I leave her punishment to him. He will tire of her, and he will curse the day he ever saw her, and sacrificed his mother and his career—everything—to a passing fancy."

"It was a terrible mistake—a—" She stopped suddenly.

"Are you ill? You look white and faint!" exclaimed Mrs Saville, roused to attention by the sudden cessation of her voice.

" Only a little giddy and dazed ; the sun was so strong to-day," returned Hope, steadying her voice by a strong effort. " I felt faint when we were driving round the lakes. But, dear Mrs Saville, may I say that greater blame attaches to the girl who allowed your son to sacrifice himself for her, than to him ? "

" No doubt she is a designing minx. But she will find that she reckoned without her host when she caught my son. Existence as the wife of a poor naval officer is not quite a bed of roses."

" And suppose she proves a devoted wife, prudent, careful, self-denying : would you not, in time, forgive her, and pardon *him* for his misfortune in falling a victim to—her designs ? "

" You suppose what is highly improbable ; but even if this woman prove a gem of the finest water, that will do

N

nothing towards pushing my son in his career. *All* must come from him; and a wife endowed with money or interest, or both, can do so much for a man. Maddening as all this is, what embitters me most is my son's contemptuous disregard of *me*. To marry without a word of notice, an attempt to win my consent was an insult."

"But, Mrs Saville, if I may venture to speak on a subject so near your heart, do you not think that the hopelessness of gaining your consent held him back from making the attempt?"

"It should have held him back also from such ungrateful disobedience. He knew he would break—no, not break my heart —mine is not the kind of heart which breaks—but harden it with a hardness that pains, with a dull, indescribable aching." And she pressed her hand on her bosom.

"Oh, yes, it was wrong — terribly wrong," cried Hope, and there was a sound of tears in her voice, "but you know your son's nature (I have heard all about his unfortunate marriage from Miss Rawson). Rightly or wrongly, he loved this girl with all his heart, and she was singularly desolate, friendless, penniless. How could he desert her, being the man he is? How could he help her effectually save as her husband? It was imprudent, I know, and very wrong, but not unpardonable. Dear Mrs Saville, think how unhappy your son must be, parted from you as he is, and, oh, think of the sad future of self-reproach and regret you are creating for his unhappy wife."

"Do not talk such sentimental rubbish to me, Miss Desmond. It is not like your usual quiet good sense. Has Mr

Rawson placed you with me to plead Hugh's cause? If so, it is wasted ingenuity. I will not be talked over; nor does Hugh think it worth while to make any attempt at reconciliation."

"Probably he fears it would only embitter you were he to try."

"No; it is pride and obstinacy. He has something of my own nature. How proud I was of him once!"

"And so you will be again," cried Hope, cheerfully. "Foolish, faulty, he may be, but he has done nothing unworthy of a man of honour. Does a marriage of affection incapacitate a man from distinguishing himself in his profession? Do you not believe that when the heart is satisfied and at rest, the intellect works more freely and clearly?"

"And do you think that the heart

will long rest satisfied when the lot of
its owner is poverty and obscurity?
There, that is enough. I will not hear
excuses or pleading for my son. If I
thought Mr Rawson suggested such interference, I would beg you to leave me
at once."

"Which I can do to-morrow, if you
wish," said Hope, her pale cheek flush-
ing quickly, though she spoke with a
pleasant smile.

Mrs Saville laughed. "You know I
should not like you to leave me," she
said, more genially than Hope once
thought she could ever speak. "Nor
need you do so, if you will avoid vexed
questions." Hope bent her head. "Tell
me," resumed Mrs Saville, "if you did
leave me, what should you do?"

"I am not absolutely without re-
sources," returned Hope, "and I should

try to find pupils or some similar employment to this."

" But you would prefer staying where you are ? "

" Yes, very, very much."

" There is a tone of sincerity in your words. Pray read to me for a while, and let us have no more agitations."

This long-wished-for opening appeared to Hope to have done very little good. She wrote an account of it to Mr Rawson. Indeed, her correspondence with the Rawson family was very constant. Every week a thick letter went to Miss Rawson, and every week came a punctual reply. Sometimes these letters sent Hope to her daily task with a soft, happy smile on her lips; sometimes her quick-falling tears bedewed the paper as she read. But, through smiles and tears, she never failed in her duty to her employer, who grew more and more dependent on her daughterly care and attention.

Mrs Saville had invited some friends who were passing through Paris to dine with her that day, so Hope felt no compunction about leaving her alone, though she was by no means anxious to accompany Miss Dacre, whose constant confidences about Lumley made her feel uncomfortable; for, during his visit to Dresden, she had perceived what was the real attraction which brought him there, and she had a sense of guilt towards Miss Dacre which oppressed her.

"However, she will be going away soon," was her reflection as she dressed, always in black, but not now in such mourning—black lace over black satin, her snowy neck and arms showing through their transparent covering, and a jet comb shining among the abundant coils of her rich, dark-chestnut hair.

"I am so glad you could come!" cried Miss Dacre, when she got into the carriage. "I cannot go quite by myself, and there is no one else in Paris I care to have. Do you know, my father says he thinks he saw George Lumley on the Boulevards this morning."

"Indeed! Well, we have seen nothing of him."

The house was crowded with a brilliant audience. The music was light and sparkling. Many glasses were turned to the box occupied by the two distinguished-looking Englishwomen. Hope Desmond had had a budget from her faithful friend Miss Rawson that evening, and something in the contents had sent her forth with a bright colour and a smiling face. Even Miss Dacre, self-absorbed as she usually was, thought, "How handsome Hope is looking!"

That young lady, who had been sweeping the house with her opera-glass, suddenly started, and exclaimed, "Why, there is George Lumley in the balcony opposite! He is with Lord Everton. Is it not extraordinary?—as soon as I come to Paris he appears. Stay! he sees us they are coming over. I don't know how it is, but I *felt* I should meet him here."

In a few minutes the door of the box opened to admit Lord Everton and his young nephew.

"Well, Miss Dacre, this is an unexpected pleasure," said the gallant old peer. "I met Castleton a couple of hours ago, and he told me you were coming here to-night. Then this young scapegrace called at my eyry *au qua-*

trième, and we agreed to look you up."

"I saw Richard Saville in town the day before yesterday," said Captain Lumley as he shook hands with Miss Desmond. "He told me you were in Paris ; and—here I am."

"It is the best time for Paris, everything looks so bright and gay," she returned, with some slight embarrassment. "Rather different from Dresden."

"I hope there may be a change from the Dresden tone," he replied, with some significance. Then he turned to greet Miss Dacre with great cordiality, and while they talked with much animation, Lord Everton addressed Miss Desmond.

"Delighted to see you ! So glad you have not deserted my distinguished sister-in-law. You remind me of Una and the Lion, or I might say the Tiger. The

softening power you have exercised is
amazing.   I only wish the process ex-
tended in widening circles to embrace a
few more than your favoured self."

"I wish I possessed the power you
credit me with," returned Hope, smiling,
as she made room for him beside her.
She was always amused with the boyish
old peer, who showed her a degree of
kindly attention which touched her.

"And how are you getting on?" he
continued, in a confidential tone.   "I
know that good fellow Rawson counted
on you as an ally in the cause of
Madame's prodigal son."

"I do not get on at all. I have had
but one chance of pleading for him, and
I am afraid I made little or no impression. Mrs Saville has been profoundly
offended. Naturally, she will find it hard
to forgive."

"She is somewhat adamantine. If you succeed with her I shall say you are a deucedly clever young woman. Still, I am inclined to back you. I must tell Hugh what a first-rate advocate he has. I had a letter from him a few days ago. His ship will be out of commission—let me see, in less than five months. The present First Lord is an old schoolfellow of mine, and he wants a lift with him. He must keep up, you know, now he is a married man—poor beggar! Then, in a way, I am responsible for his sins."

"Oh, indeed!" said Hope, looking at him with eager, earnest eyes.

"Yes; I knew old Hilton for years, off and on. He wasn't a bad fellow at all—very much in my own line; and I am not at all a bad fellow, I assure you."

"I am sure you are not," returned Hope, with a caressing smile.

"What a sweet soul you are to say so!" showing all his still white teeth in a genial laugh. "Then he, Hugh, met the daughter—an uncommon girl, I believe, sang divinely, and all that."

"Did you know her *too?*" asked Hope.

"Well, I have seen her, years ago, when she was in short frocks with a pigtail. Then she was away in England for some time, but Hilton did not consider it prudent to cross the Channel. Anyhow, Hugh is most anxious about his precious wife, and fears she may get into trouble during his absence. I am thinking of running down to Nice to look her up. She is there still, isn't she?"

"I think—that is, Mr Rawson thinks

she has left. You had better ask him."

"I will," with some significance. "May I call upon her imperious Highness, do you think?"

"I can hardly tell. You might leave a card. I am inclined to think that she would be pleased by your kind effort to further her son's interest."

"That is a little encouraging. Hugh has always been a favourite of mine. He is a fine fellow, and I do not think he will revenge himself on the poor girl who is the innocent cause of his misfortunes. Gad! a sweet charming woman is worth paying dear for!"—a sentiment which seemed to touch his hearer, for she gave him a soft, lingering, tearful glance, which, "had I been some twenty years younger," thought the old boy, "I should have felt inclined to repay with a kiss."

Meantime, Miss Dacre's bright beady eyes danced in her head with delight as she chattered volubly to Lumley, whose face grew rather sulky as he listened, scarcely deigning to reply. Here a welcome interruption came in the shape of one of the English attachés, for whom Lumley immediately vacated his seat; and, as Lord Everton wished to say a word to one of the singers, he departed behind the scenes, and Lumley slipped into his place.

"My uncle was fortunate in securing your devoted attention, Miss Desmond."

"Yes; he always interests me."

"Lucky old fellow! What have you been doing with yourself?" continued Lumley, looking earnestly at her. "You are looking pale and thin, and your eyes—"

Hope interrupted him by holding up

a finger. "What a rude speech," she exclaimed.

"You ought to know by this time that I am too deeply interested in you to pay you compliments."

"And *you* ought to know by this time, Captain Lumley, that I am an ungrateful creature, and not deserving of your interest."

"Whether you deserve it or not, I can't help feeling it."

"Has Mr Saville any thoughts of coming to Paris?"

"I don't know. He will probably pay his respected mamma a visit. He is at present deeply engaged assisting a desperate female antiquarian who is collecting materials for the history of Queen Bertha, or Boadicea, or some such remote potentate. Whether she will end by leading him to the hymeneal

altar is uncertain ; but it is quite possible."

" I earnestly hope poor Mrs Saville
may be spared this last straw," exclaimed
Hope, smiling.

"I am sure I don't care. I only care
for my own troubles. I have been the
most miserable beggar in existence for
the last four or five months, hoping and
fearing, and dragged every way. I am
resolved to put an end to this infernal
uncertainty and know my fate. Don't
you think I am right?"

"How can I tell?" Hope was beginning, when Miss Dacre broke in : "You
will come back to sup with me, will you
not, Miss Desmond? Captain Lumley
and Lord Everton are coming, and Lady
Delamere, and Monsieur de la Taille. I
will send my maid home with you
after."

O

"Many thanks, Miss Dacre, I really must not." An animated argument followed; but Hope Desmond stuck to her resolution, and, declining Captain Lumley's proffered escort, drove back to Meurice's alone.

Mrs Saville was rather amused in Paris; she met many acquaintances who did not bore her, and she tolerated Captain Lumley's visits more good-humouredly than formerly, chiefly because he was quiet and *distrait*.

About a week after Hope had gone to the opera with Miss Dacre, Mrs Saville had gone to drive in the Bois with an invalid dowager duchess who was on her way to some famous health-resort in Switzerland, and Hope, having finished her weekly letter, went out to post it proceeding afterwards to do some shopping. On her way back, near the Théâtre

Français, she met Lumley, who immediately turned with her. They walked rather silently to the hotel, Hope feeling very anxious to get rid of him, yet somehow deterred from acting with decision, but a certain air of resolution by no means usual which pervaded his face and voice seemed to hold her back.

"Has Mrs Saville returned?" asked Hope of the waiter who attended their suite of rooms.

"Not yet, mademoiselle," he replied.

"Then—" she began, holding out her hand to Lumley; but he did not take it.

"If you will allow me, I will come in and wait for her," he said, with so much decision that she felt it would be easier to let him come in than to resist. He therefore followed her upstairs to the pleasant *salon* looking out on the Tuileries gardens, where Hope took off her hat, intending to supply him with a newspaper and leave him to his own reflections. This plan was nipped in the bud.

Having walked to the window and looked out for a minute, Lumley returned and closed the door. Standing between it and Hope, he said, very quietly, "This is the first chance I have had of speaking to you, and I implore you to hear me. I insist on your hearing me. You have treated me with the most insulting indifference, and obstinately refused to understand the feelings I have tried to show you. Now I am determined to speak out. I am madly in love with you. I would sacrifice everything and every one for you. I am desperately in earnest. Promise that you will love me, that you will even try to love me, and I'll—I'll marry

you to-morrow, No! hear me further,"
as Hope attempted to speak. "Just
think of the different life you would
lead with me. You would have society,
position, freedom. We might be obliged
to pinch at first, but nothing can keep
the family estates from me when my
father is gone; and I could always get
money. Then compare life with a husband who adores you, with that of a
sort of upper servant to a cantankerous,
dictatorial, tyrannical old woman like
my Aunt Saville. You must not refuse
me, Hope. I'll blow out my brains if
you do." He tried to catch her hand,
which she quickly snatched away, stepping back a space or two, while she
grew alternately pale and red under the
passionate gaze of the eager young
man.

"Now, *you* must listen to *me*, Captain

Lumley. You have distressed me infinitely. You ought to have understood by my manner that I wished to avoid such an explanation—to save you, as well as myself, the pain it must cause. It is impossible that I could love you as you wish. And it is well I do not; for there is no reason why you should grieve your parents as your cousin has done his mother."

"That need not weigh with you," cried Lumley. "I wrote to my father yesterday, and told him I should ask you, and if you accepted me, as I hoped you would, nothing should prevent our marriage."

"How insane of you!" said Hope, greatly agitated. "Why could you not see that I should never under any circumstances have loved you, we are so unlike in every way?"

"That's no reason why we should not be perfectly happy; and see all I can give you."

"All you could give has not a feather's weight with me. I am profoundly grieved that I could not keep you from this mortification. You will find many good and charming women, who, if you seek them, would love you well; and I will even tell you that I have no heart to give. I am engaged to a man I love with all my soul, and no one can put him out of my mind."

"Who and what is he?" cried Lumley, fiercely, starting forward from where he had been leaning against the window-frame.

"I will tell you so much. He is poor like myself, and we have a long struggle before us, but— There, I will say no more. Now that you understand there is no hope, you will be able to put me out of your thoughts. Do tell your father he has nothing to fear, at least from me. It is cruel to disappoint a father, a parent. See what suffering Hugh Saville had caused his mother."

"By heaven, he was right. He got what he wanted. I am infernally disappointed. I thought when you knew what I really meant, you—"

"It is useless to argue about what is inevitable," interrupted Hope, with some *hauteur.* "I deeply regret having caused you annoyance or disappointment, but neither you nor I would have been happy if we had become man and wife. Why, oh, why did you not understand me? Now I can hear no more. Make haste to relieve your father's mind, and —good-bye, Captain Lumley." She half put out her hand, drew it back, and left

the room swiftly. The enraged and disappointed lover took a turn to and fro,
uttering some half - articulate denuncia-
tions of his infernal ill luck, then,
snatching up his hat, rushed away to
pour his troubles into the sympathising
ear of Lord Everton, in whom all
imprudent youngsters found a congenial
confidant.

As soon as the sound of his steps was
heard, the unclosed door of a small inner
room, from which there was no other
exit, and which was used as a *cabinet
d'écriture*, was pushed more widely open,
and Mrs Saville walked in. She wore
her out-door dress, and held a note in
her hand.

"I little thought what I should hear,"
she said, almost aloud, "when I determined to keep quiet till that booby had
gone. Listeners never hear good of

themselves.   So I am a cantankerous,
dictatorial, tyrannical old woman ?   Hope
Desmond does not think so; I know
she does not."

CHAPTER IX

To Hope, Mrs Saville made no sign, and
she remained in complete ignorance that
her acute patroness had been a hearer
of Lumley's avowal.

There was something increasingly kind
and confidential, however, in her tone
and manner. Hope was greatly relieved
by having thus disposed of her admirer.
That worry was at an end; another,
however, still remained.

Miss Dacre's feelings and imagination
were greatly exercised by the sudden
disappearance of George Lumley from
the scene, and she grew quite ravenous
for Hope's society, that she might wonder

and conjecture and maunder about his mysterious conduct, and cross-examine Hope as to what *she* thought might, could, would or should have caused him thus suddenly to throw up the game which Miss Dacre chose to think he was playing so eagerly—viz., the pursuit of herself—till she made her hearer's life a burden to her.

"I don't know what you do to Miss Desmond when you have her out by herself," said Mrs Saville to the young heiress one afternoon, when she had called to know if dear Mrs Saville would spare Hope Desmond to take a drive with her and stay to afternoon tea, "but she always comes back looking white and tired, quite exhausted; and I will *not* spare her, Miss Dacre. I want her myself. If you are always taking her away, you had better keep her."

"I am sure I shall be delighted. I want a nice lady-like companion a little older than myself, to go about with me, and—"

"A little older than yourself!" laughed Mrs Saville. "I suspect she is two years your junior. Well, take her if she will go."

"Indeed, Mrs Saville, I think you would do better with an older person, some one nearer your own age."

"I am much obliged for your kind consideration. Yes, of course Miss Desmond has rather a dull time with me. Suppose you make her an offer in writing."

"Yes, of course I could; that is, if you would not be offended."

"No, by no means. I would not stand in her light."

"Really, Mrs Saville, you are the

most sensible woman I know. Pray, how much do you give her?—what salary, I mean?"

"What Mr Rawson asked for his *protégée*—fifty pounds."

"Is that all? Oh, I will give her a hundred."

"Then, of course, you will get her," said Mrs Saville grimly. "That being so, pray leave her to me for this afternoon."

"Oh, yes, certainly. I can write to her this evening." Her further utterance was arrested by the announcement, in loud tones, of Lady Olivia Lumley, whereupon that personage entered, wearing a simple travelling-dress and a most troubled expression of countenance.

"Dear Miss Dacre, I had no idea I should find you here," said Lady Olivia, when she had greeted Mrs Saville. "I am on my way to Contrexéville, to try

and get rid of my gouty rheumatism:
so—"

"How very unfortunate that Captain
Lumley should just have left!" interrupted Miss Dacre. "He started on
Wednesday — something regimental I
believe."

"Most unfortunate," returned Lady
Olivia, emphatically.

"Where are you staying?" asked Miss
Dacre.

"At the Hôtel d'Albe."

"Well, I shall call late this afternoon.
Now, I am obliged to call on the
Comtesse de Surèsnes. So good-bye for
the present, Mrs Saville. Good-bye,
dear Lady Olivia."

As soon as she was gone, Mrs Saville,
looking very straight at her sister-in-law,
asked, "What is the matter with
you?"

"Matter! Matter enough! If I had not been *en route* for Contrexéville I should have come here on purpose to—to tell you what I think."

"And pray what may that be, Lady Olivia?"

"That you have allowed my unfortun-ate boy George to fall into the same scrape as your own son, just to make *us* suffer as you have done. It is *too* bad, that while we were thinking everything was on the point of being settled be-tween him and Mary Dacre (such an excellent marriage), there is he falling into the trap of that low-born, designing adventuress your companion! You are not a woman to be blinded by anything, and you never took the trouble to warn us or save him, and I who always sympathised with you in your trouble about Hugh! I expected better things from you, Elizabeth. You are infatuated about that woman, of whom you really know nothing."

For a moment Mrs Saville was silent, too amazed to find words.

"I don't understand you. Pray explain your meaning, if you have any," she said at last, a bitter little smile curling up the corners of her mouth.

"Why, our unfortunate, mad boy wrote to his father a few days ago that he was going to make an offer to that dreadful girl, as she was the sort of woman to whom he dared not propose a private marriage; that he feared we might be vexed at first, but if we attempted to prevent it he would go straight to the dogs. Oh, it is too— too bad. I little thought, when I was so horrified at Hugh's conduct last summer, that before a year was over

P

I should be afflicted in the same way."

"When you gloated over my disappointment, you mean," cried Mrs Saville, her keen black eyes flashing. "I have no doubt you thought to yourself that *your* son would never be false to the instincts of his race, which is aristocratic on *both* sides, but that *mine* was impelled by the plebeian vigour inherited from his mother's people. *I* know the amount of gratitude you all feel towards *me* for conferring wealth, for which he never toiled, on your brother and his sons. But the blood in my veins has been strong enough to keep you all in your places. Yes! as the world *we* live in chooses to attach importance to rank and to worship a title, I bought what was necessary of the valuable article; but I know *your* estimate of me and the

veiled contempt of your commiseration
when the blow fell upon me. Now I am
going to return good for evil, and
relieve your mind. Your precious son
is perfectly safe. That low-born, designing adventuress my companion has de-
fiantly and utterly rejected him."

"Impossible! Are you sure? May
this not be some deep-laid scheme?
How do you know?"

"It is quite possible, I am perfectly
sure; it is no deep-laid scheme, I know,
because I was in that room there, un-
suspected, and heard every word of the
proposal and of the distinct, decided
rejection. Miss Desmond reproached
your son with his perseverance in spite
of her discouragement, and informed him
she was engaged to another—evidently
some humble, struggling man, from
whom your charming, distinguished son

was powerless to attract her. Miss Desmond acted like a young woman of sense and honour, and in my opinion she is a great deal too good even for so high and mighty a gentleman as Captain George Lumley."

"Thank God!" cried Lady Olivia, too much relieved to resent the undisguised scorn and anger of her sister-in-law. "But are you quite sure there is no danger of this—young person changing her mind?"

"Be under no apprehension. Your son is safe enough so far as my young friend Miss Desmond is concerned."

"I am sure I am very glad; but really, Elizabeth, I am amazed at the very extraordinary attack you have made upon me."

"Or, rather, you are amazed that I know you so well. I saw the sneer that lurked under your assumed compassion for my disappointment, and I am amazed you ventured to speak in the tone you did to me. Now you may go, and write to your husband and assure him his son is safe for the present. Before we meet again, you must apologise to me for the liberty you have taken."

"I think an apology is also due to me," cried Lady Olivia.

While she spoke, Mrs Saville had rung the bell, and, on the waiter's appearance, said, in a commanding tone, "Lady Olivia Lumley's carriage," whereupon that lady confessed defeat by retiring rapidly.

Mrs Saville walked to her special arm-chair, and, taking Prince into her lap, stroked him mechanically, as was her wont when she was thinking.

"So *that* was the fool's attraction?" she mused. "I ought to have suspected

it, but I did not, or I should have sent
him about his business. It is natural
enough that the father and mother should
be annoyed ; but she is too good for him
—a great deal too good. But she is silly,
too, with her high - flown notions. We
cannot defy the judgment and prejudices
of the world we live in ; obscurity and
insignificance are abhorrent to most sane
people. Yet it is impossible to doubt
her sincerity ; and she is common-sensical
enough. Can it be that she is wise and
I am *unwise?*" Here Mrs Saville put
her little favourite on the carpet and
again rang the bell. This time she desired that Miss Desmond should be sent
to her.

"I think I shall go out and do some
shopping," she said, when Hope appeared.
"I do not walk enough. I have had
a tiresome morning. First Miss Dacre

came begging that you might be lent to
her for the day. This I refused. Then
came Lady Olivia, in a bad temper,
and we quarrelled. She is going away
to-morrow or next day. At all events,
she shall not trouble me any more.
I think we have had enough of Paris.
Richard is coming over next week. As
soon as he leaves, I shall go away
to a quaint little place on the coast of
Normandy, and recruit. It will be very
dull, but you are used to that."

"I rarely feel dull," returned Hope,
who secretly wondered why Mrs Saville
had quarrelled with her sister-in-law.
She was too decided, too peremptory a
woman to be quarrelsome. Could it be
for any reason connected with herself?
Lumley said he had communicated his
intention to propose for her (Hope) to
his father. This, no doubt, would have

enraged his family; but she could not ask any questions. Indeed, she was thankful to "let sleeping dogs lie." She had many anxieties pressing on her young heart. A very cloudy and uncertain future lay before her. "It is hard," she thought, "that, however good and true and loving a woman may be, if not rich, she is thought unworthy to be the helpmate of a wealthy, well-placed man; any poor, struggling nobody is good enough for her. Yet it is among the struggling nobodies that the finest fellows are often found: so things equalise themselves."

That evening, as Hope was playing some Scotch airs, with great taste and a delicate touch, while Mrs Saville sat thinking in her chair and stroking Prince, a note was brought for Miss Desmond. Hope finished what she was playing, then asking, "Will you allow me?" opened the missive.

"It is from Miss Dacre," she added, in a minute or two—"a most extraordinary epistle. She says she writes with your knowledge and approval. She asks me to leave you and live with her, and offers me one hundred pounds a year. Will you look at it."

Mrs Saville stretched out her hand, and, after reading the letter, deliberately returned it.

"How do you mean to reply?"

"Can you ask?" cried Hope—"unless, indeed, your knowledge of Miss Dacre's intention indicates a wish that I should leave you."

"No, it does not. I thought it right that you should have the option of refusing an advantageous offer. You would have more gaiety, a larger salary, an easier life with Mary Dacre than with a cantankerous old woman like myself."

"If I had the money I should be willing to pay a hundred a year to stay away from Miss Dacre," said Hope. "You are severe, and rather formidable, but I feel sure of your justice and loyalty, and the restfulness of life with you is infinitely preferable to the fevered gaiety of Miss Dacre's existence."

"I am glad you think so. Write to her at once."

Hope obeyed, and, after writing with deliberation for some minutes, gave the result to Mrs Saville for perusal.

"Good," said that lady. "It is firm and courteous. Let it be posted at once. Now play me the march from 'Tannhäuser.'"

When that was finished, Mrs Saville said, "Come and sit down."

Hope obeyed. There was a short pause, and she went on : " As you have chosen so stay with me, my dear Miss Desmond, I shall increase your salary to what Miss Dacre offered."

" You are very good, Mrs Saville, but I would rather you did not. I have quite enough for all I want. A year hence, when you have proved me, if we are still together, and you like to offer it— But, oh ! it is unwise to look ahead so far."

" I am not a very imaginative person," said Mrs Saville, slowly, "but it strikes me you have a history, Miss Desmond."

" I suppose every one has," said Hope, smiling. " I, too, have my little story, and some day, if you ever care to hear it, I will tell you—but not just yet."

"I suppose it centres round some love affair, which you silly young people always think of the last importance."

"It does," said Hope, with grave feeling; "and I am sure the importance cannot be exaggerated. If men and women only allowed themselves to think what a sacred and solemn thing love, and its usual ending, marriage, is, fewer unhappy ones would take place."

"Ah, with the vast majority love is an unknown quantity and an insignificant ingredient. Just think what human nature is, the conditions in which it lives, moves and has its being; how is love, as you exalted people accept it, to exist? There, we shall never agree. Pray get me the *Figaro.*"

Miss Dacre was reproachful, and even tearful, when Hope next saw her, but

the "much desired one" was im-
movable.

"Is it not extraordinary," cried the disappointed heiress, "that George Lumley
went off in that unaccountable way?
There is some hidden, baneful influence
at work. It is always the same; as soon
as we are growing confidential he flies
off. It is a hideous thought, but it *has*
occurred to me that he is secretly
married to some dreadful woman. What
do *you* think?"

"I think there is nothing more
unlikely."

"Heaven grant it! Well, good-bye.
We return to London on Wednesday.
Perhaps Richard Saville will be able to
tell me something of George. Oh, I
forget: we shall just miss him. Well, if
you can find out anything you will be
sure to write? You have treated me

very badly; but I do not bear malice. You will find you have made a great mistake. So good-bye."

Mrs Saville seemed more cheerful and in a better temper after Lord Castleton and his daughter left Paris, though the presence of her eldest son was always more or less a trial.

She endured an occasional visit from Lord Everton, who was quietly pertinacious in cultivating friendly relations with her.

He was the only member of the family who dared to mention her offending son, but he only ventured to do so when they were alone.

"I really believe you are softening Mrs Saville's stony heart," he said one day as he met Hope coming from the galleries (not the Grands Magasins) of the Louvre. "Not I am sure, *à la mode de Hannibal,*

by fire and vinegar, but rather with the
milk of human kindness. She allows me
to mention Hugh, and just now endured
hearing that I had a letter from him.
He writes in good spirits. I believe the
Vortigern will be home in August or
September, and then we shall see what
we shall see—oh, allow me," for Hope
had dropped her sunshade and stooped
to pick it up. "Getting quite too hot
to stay here. I am off to Switzerland;
and I hear Richard is going to cruise in
somebody's yacht to the coast of Norway.
He has scent of some buried treasures
of Runic inscriptions, and heaven knows
what else, near Skarstad. You had
better get Mrs Saville away, and yourself too. You are looking pale and
seedy—excuse a privileged old fellow.
You have my best wishes, my dear girl
—my very best. Accept a prophecy:

I *think* we'll turn a corner before long."

And before Hope could ask the meaning of his enigmatical words he had raised his hat, bowed and departed.

CHAPTER X

THE little fishing-village of Sainte-Croix, lying at the mouth of a valley or gorge which opens from the sea between high cliffs on the coast of Normandy, has of late been revealed to Parisians, especially artistic and literary Parisians. One giant of the latter order has even built himself a villa well up on the steep side of the valley   Artists encamp in the fisher cottages, turning the kitchens, with their carved oak dressers and settles, into living-rooms, and cooking in outhouses, or getting their food from a rambling hotel and restaurant lately instituted by joining several cottages together, with

Q

additions and improvements, where a few yards of level ground intervene between the sands and the cliff.

A straggling growth of fine beech-trees stretches down from a large wood which crowns the gradual ascent of the valley, where it merges into the flat table-land above, well cultivated, and rich with fields of corn and colza. At the date of this story it was known to few, but, obscure though it was, Mrs Saville chose it for a resting-place before she returned to London. It was a fine glowing August evening when, with Miss Desmond, her German courier, and her English maid, Mrs Saville arrived and startled the sleepy little village into lively curiosity, as she drove through it in an old-fashioned travelling-carriage drawn by four scraggy post-horses, the whole equipage secured with some difficulty by the careful courier

at the nearest railway-station. The dogs
barked, the hens cackled, the ducks and
geese flew out of the roadside pond with
prodigious noise and flutterings, as the
scarecrow team rattled down the hill to
the shore of the rock-encircled bay along
the edge of which the "Hôtel de l'Europe"
stretched its low, irregular front.

The landlord and one male and two
female waiters were drawn up to receive
the distinguished guests and usher them
to their apartments.

"Madame has a fine view of the bay
and cliffs. The sunsets are superb, nay,
exquisite, in good weather; and it is
generally good at Sainte-Croix. I do not
remember having had the honour of
receiving Madame before."

"I dare say not. You were not old
enough to be the head of such an establish-
ment when I was here last," returned Mrs

Saville, more graciously than she would
have spoken to an Englishman.

"Impossible, Madame!" cried the host,
with polite incredulity. "When will
Madame dine?"

"At six. Meantime, we want tea; but
my courier will see to the preparation.
He understands it. Pray, is Madame
d'Albeville at the château?"

"No, madame. Unfortunately, the
second son of Madame la Marquise was
wounded a week ago in a duel, and she
has gone to nurse him—at Grenoble, I
think. Her arrival is quite uncertain."

"Indeed! I am sorry to hear it."
And she bowed dismissal to her polite
host.

"This is a disappointment," said Mrs
Saville to Hope. "I quite counted on
Madame d'Albeville's society. She is an
agreeable, sensible woman, and rather

pleasantly associated with my former visit to this little hamlet. Come, let us look at our rooms."

They were small, but more comfortable than the guests had anticipated. Hope was greatly pleased with the picturesque surroundings, and was anxious to survey the village.

"Then take Jessop with you for a ramble. I have letters to write, and do not feel inclined to move. Tell them to light a fire in the *salon*. I like a fire and open windows. The air is very fresh and deliciously salt, but I can quite bear a fire."

Hope willingly accepted the suggestion, and as soon as they had a cup of tea she set out with the prosaic lady's-maid, glad to enjoy some exercise after the long, cramping journey by rail and road.

It was indeed a primitive little place.

A narrow, stony road led between two irregular lines of detached cottages, each with a little garden, many of them overgrown with ivy and roses. Frequent steep paths between them led to huts perched on the hill-sides above them. Gradually the road climbed up clear of these surroundings to where on the higher ground the ruins of a mediæval abbey peeped out from the shelter of the surrounding beech woods. Hope and her companion did not venture quite so far, but even from the height they had attained they looked out over the blue waters of the Channel, now glittering and laughing in the strong light of the westering sun.

"We must return now, Jessop," said Hope. "Mrs Saville will have been a long time alone by the time we get back."

"She will indeed, miss; and what made Mrs Saville come to this savage place is past my comprehension," returned the abigail, in an aggrieved tone. "There seems to be nothing but common people without shoes to their feet going about. I am sure Mrs Saville would have got her health better at Inglefield, with the comforts and decencies as become her station around her."

"Perhaps so; but this is a sweet place. I think I could enjoy it intensely, if— if—" She paused, and her rich red lips parted in an unconscious smile.

"If your young gentleman was here, miss?" said Jessop, with a confidential smirk. Jessop had grown friendly and slightly patronising to her lady's young companion.

Hope laughed, and the yearning of her heart prompted her to reply, "Yes, that would make it a heavenly place, Jessop; but I must not allow myself to think of such joy."

"That's a pity, miss. So there *is* a young gentleman? Indeed, I'd be surprised if there was not. I hope he isn't too far away, miss?"

"Yes, there is many a weary mile between us."

"That's bad, miss. Men are an inconstant lot; it's out of sight out of mind with the most of them. *I* was engaged once myself, to a young gentleman in the grocery line, but he behaved most treacherous, and married a butcher's daughter. She was freckled and cross-eyed, but she had a tidy bit of money; and a man would marry the witch of Endor for that."

"I dare say the witch of Endor was a very attractive woman."

" Law, miss ! an old witch ? "

" Oh, no ; a nice witch is never old."

Here this intellectual conversation was interrupted by the sound of approaching wheels, and the pound, pound, crunch, crunch, of a patient, heavy-footed horse toiling slowly up-hill.

Hitherto the place had been so silent, so apparently deserted, that both Hope and her attendant paused and looked anxiously down the road, which made a sharp bend at the point from which they had begun to walk back. The sounds of a deep, rough voice, uttering obser-vations in an unknown tongue which seemed hawked up from the pit of the speaker's stomach, next made themselves heard ; presently appeared a tall, thin .man, clad in holland overall trousers, a dark-brown knitted waistcoat, and a holland jacket, neither of the lighter garments

having lately seen the wash-tub ; a wide-
brimmed straw hat, turned up at the
back, projected far over his eyes, which,
as he looked up, showed black and pierc-
ing under bushy, grizzled eyebrows. Long,
lantern jaws, thick untrimmed moustaches,
and a skin like wrinkled leather, gave
him the air of a countrified Pantaloon.
Behind him came a broad-chested grey
horse, almost white from age, his harness
much mended with rope, and a long
fore-lock falling into his eyes. He was
drawing an old, rusty, ramshackle cabrio-
let, the hood drawn forward and nod-
ding at every step of the *attelage.* He
was led by an old, thickset man in a blue
blouse and a cloth cap pulled down
nearly over his ears. As the first of the
curious couple approached them, he raised
his straw hat with an air of much elegance
to Hope and her companion, wishing

them *bonsoir* in a well-bred voice, and held his hat aloft till he was quite past.

"Well, that *is* a guy!" exclaimed Jessop. "I am sure he would not do for any one's young man, even in a desert like this. He'd want the witch of Endor to keep him company, he would."

"I was rather interested by his face," said Hope. "He has a most expressive countenance, and fine eyes."

"Law, miss! I wonder what your young gentleman would say to your taste?"

"And I wonder who he is?" continued Hope.

"I dare say I shall soon find out at the hotel," returned Jessop. "And now we had better step out, for I am sure my mistress does not like being left too long by herself."

Hope found Mrs Saville surrounded by pens, ink and paper; she had evidently been busy with her pen, for a number of freshly-stamped letters lay beside her, and the hearth was cumbered with a large amount of charred fragments. Moreover, Mrs Saville did not seem aware that Hope had been long absent, and was much surprised when the head-waiter announced, "Madame est servie."

The sunset that evening justified the landlord's eulogium, and Mrs Saville gazed at it long in deep thought. It was perhaps a contradiction in her rather complicated nature that she enjoyed fine scenery — indeed, beauty in any shape. This she said very little about, as she looked upon such tendencies as indicative of weakness. Suddenly she turned to Hope and said, " I remember just such a sunset over this little bay nearly twenty years ago, when Hugh was a little fellow, and in all those years he was a satisfac-

tion to me till—till he destroyed my
hopes forever. We had been travelling,
and I wanted to see the old Norman
churches. There are some very fine
specimens of Gothic in this part of
the country. We stopped for a day or
two at Caen, when Hugh, who was with
me for his holiday-time, showed symptoms
of fever. They advised me to take him
to Sainte-Croix, where the air was pure
and bracing. He was wonderfully happy
here. Madame d'Albeville was then at
the château. I had known her brother
in London. He was one of the French
attachés. He happened to be at the
château too. They found me out, and
were wonderfully kind. It is one of the
few purely pleasant memories I have,
those weeks. The Marquise and I never
quite lost sight of each other since.
When we were in Paris she told me she

would be here all July and August. It
is a great disappointment not to find
her here."

"I can understand that," said Hope,
softly. Her lips trembled as she spoke,
and her eyes dwelt with a strained,
anxious expression on the delicate, strong
face of her patroness.

She began again in a quiet tone, as
if unconscious of Hope's presence : " Poor
Hugh ! He has earned his own punishment. I am glad I destroyed my last
will." And she glanced at the fireplace.
Then, suddenly addressing Hope, "You
will be glad too. You seem to have
espoused his cause. Mr Rawson was
always devoted to Hugh, and you have
caught his enthusiasm. That parcel
which came to me before we left Paris
from Rawson's office was my will. I
wanted to read it. I thought of add-

ing a codicil, but I could not make up my mind. I had dreamed of that will, and struggled with my heart, my pride. This afternoon, as I sat alone, I seemed to see Hugh, to hear his voice, and the impulse came on me; I thrust the paper that doomed him to poverty into the fire. It is done with." She paused.

Hope could not speak.

"But I am not going to leave him more than a competence; no, he does not deserve that I should give him ease of circumstance; but I have a 'will' form with me, and to-morrow I will fill it up. I have planned what I shall put in it. I will not be harsh; I will be just."

"And you will be ever so much happier, dear Mrs Saville."

"Happy! Do you know, I doubt if I know what happiness is?"

"That is very extraordinary."

"Is it? Have you known much happiness?"

Hope seemed to think for a moment, then an indescribable sweetness, a sudden light, came into her eyes.

"I have known glimpses of *great* happiness; of smaller happiness, often; of bitterness and sadness, now and then."

"A varied experience for so young a woman. By the way, I never think of you as a girl; yet you are quite young —I see and feel that. Now let us read the English papers which came this evening. I was glad to see them; for the post at these out-of-the-way places is always uncertain."

The next day, however, Mrs Saville did not feel equal to write or attend to business. Her head felt heavy and giddy, she said: so she ordered the

ramshackle carriage and drove to the
château, hoping the air would revive
her. It did not, however. She said
she felt inclined to sleep—that the air
was too strong for her, or rather that
she had grown too weak for the air—
that the place made her melancholy,
and she would leave next day. Hope
persuaded her to try and rest. She
covered her over with wraps; for,
though the day was warm, she complained of cold, and shivered a good
deal. Hope took her knitting and sat
patiently beside her for more than an
hour, during which Mrs Saville slept
heavily, sometimes moaning; then she
woke suddenly, as if startled, and
thought she had heard several people
enter the room noisily. She was better,
and insisted on taking a little walk on
the beach. At dinner she could not eat,

R

but complained of great thirst. Feeling severe headache and drowsiness, she went early to bed. Hope felt more uneasy than she cared to confess, and persuaded Mrs Saville to let her maid sleep in her room.

Then she retired herself, first to write at considerable length, then to seek forgetfulness in her bed. But in vain; her nerves were strained, and an irresistible presentiment of evil weighed her down.

The long, wakeful, restless night wore through.

At early dawn Jessop came into Miss Desmond's room with an alarmed look on her face.

"I am afraid Mrs Saville is very ill, miss. I have never seen her like this. She has been wandering off and on all night about Mr Hugh and her husband, that no one ever hears her speak about. Just now she is asleep. What will be-

come of us in this poor, miserable place
if my lady gets really ill? Why, we
couldn't get h'ice or a doctor; though
that queer man we saw on the road
yesterday, they tell me, is a very
clever doctor, but he lives miles and
miles away."

"I shall get up and dress at once,"
returned Hope, much alarmed. "I will,
come to Mrs Saville directly"

She dressed accordingly, little thinking how long it would be before she
should again go regularly to bed.

Mrs Saville seemed quite herself when
Hope reached her bedside, except that
her hands and skin were dry and burning, her eyes bright and restless. She
refused her *café au lait*, and wanted
to get up in order to prepare for her
journey to London. She seemed fever-
ishly anxious to be at home once more.

Then she began to speak about Mr Rawson as if he were there, though they both knew he had started with his daughter for Switzerland ; also she talked of her will, and her fear that if she died intestate her son Hugh would get as much of her property as his brother.

As soon as she could get away, Hope called the landlord and begged him to despatch a mounted messenger for the doctor, to whom she hastily wrote a note describing the condition of the sufferer as accurately as she could. This done, there was nothing for it but waiting.

This waiting tried Hope severely. She felt, moreover, what a weight of responsibility lay upon her.

Though Jessop was full of expressions of sympathy and woe, her pale face and nervous manner showed how unfit she was for a sick-nurse.

Hope waited for the doctor's report before she wrote to Mr Rawson's partner for help and counsel.

Richard Saville was away cruising, nobody knew where; Mr Rawson was travelling; Lord Everton—who could find him? and she felt, she knew, that Mrs Saville was going to be very ill.

At last, after what seemed ages, but really as soon as he could come, the doctor appeared.

Though rusty and dislocated in appearance, he was kindly and intelligent. After examining his patient, he asked Hope if she was her daughter.

"A much attached friend, then?" he said, when she answered in the negative. "I fear the poor lady is seriously ill. It is rather difficult to foresee how these feverish attacks may turn, and we can only help nature. There is little to be done. I have brought medicines with me, thanks to the description in your note. Sainte-Croix boasts no chemist's shop. You must watch your patient constantly. Give her milk when you can get her to take anything. I will speak to the landlord about a few precautions which it would be as well to take, and I think you had better have a nurse—a sick-nurse—to assist you. It seems to me that Madame has been a healthy woman ? "

" Remarkably healthy, I believe."

" That is well. A reserve force of untried strength is the best help in these cases. I will come over very early to-morrow morning, and, if possible, bring a nurse with me."

So Hope was left with a sinking heart to watch the sick-bed, to administer what medicine was ordered, to cool the burning skin by applying a lotion which smelt of camphor, to pray for strength and courage. She sent the courier to the nearest telegraph-station, some miles off, to wire a message for her solicitors, describing Mrs Saville's condition, and begging that Mr Rawson and Richard Saville might be sent for.

Meantime, a note of terror had spread through the household. Some precautions suggested by the doctor gave rise to exaggerated ideas of infection, and Hope soon began to perceive that the service of the sick-room was becoming a difficulty.

The doctor was faithful to his word, and returned with a sturdy, broad-faced Sister of Mercy, who was an immense help. Then the sad routine of a sick-room was instituted. Gradually Hope came to know that the enemy with which they had to contend was severe typhus fever. The whole weight of attendance fell on Hope and the Sister. At times Mrs Saville was wildly excited, striving *to* get out of bed and wandering deliriously. In her worst state Hope's voice and touch had a certain degree of influence upon her. The weary days, and still wearier nights, dragged their slow length along. Letters came from Mr Rawson's partner assuring Miss Desmond that he was in hopes a letter would find Mr Saville in the Island of Rügen, where his bankers believed he would make a short stay, and that he had telegraphed to Mr Rawson, who ought to be at Basle on the 7th : no doubt that gentleman would lose no time in going to Sainte-Croix.

Still the days and nights rolled heavily on, and no one came.

" If all our care fails," thought Hope,

"what a terrible position for me! I have done my best; but will Mrs Saville's people think I have? If she dies unreconciled to Hugh, what a tragedy!" What moments Hope could spare from the sufferer she spent in writing, covering the pages rapidly. These letters she sent by the courier to the market-town, that they might escape the uncertainties of the Sainte-Croix post-office.

"Mademoiselle will kill herself," said Sister Marie, the nurse, one morning. "You do the work, the watching, of two. And you are imprudent: you let her hold your hand and lean against you. It is unwise. You must take some rest. Trust me a little."

"I do, dear Sister, I do. But *I* cannot rest. You do not know how my life seems to depend on hers."

"*Bon Dieu!* and you are not her daughter!"

The tenth day came, and Mrs Saville seemed sinking rapidly. The doctor remained all night. Hope sat by the bed-side. Haggard, dry-eyed, sometimes the sufferer uttered the name of her offending son, sometimes she murmured inarticulately. The eleventh day dawned grey and overcast. Hitherto the weather had been fine, and warm enough to make it difficult to keep the sick-room tolerably cool. In after years, the shimmer of moonlight on the sea, and the sweet, soothing rhythm of the soft, upward rush and backward sweep of wavelets on a pebbly beach, always brought the sick-room and the terrible anxiety of those days vividly before Hope's mind. A cooler wind now blew gently, and Hope, who had snatched half an hours

rest, came soon after dawn to resume
her watch. She was startled. Had the
proud, hard, disappointed woman passed
away? She lay so still, with something of that "rapture of repose" which
only death can bring. She looked at
the Sister—a look of terrified inquiry.
"She lives, but scarcely breathes," was
the whispered reply. Hope bent over
the bed, and touched the thin hand
which lay outside the clothes. "She *is*
breathing regularly. Her hand is not
burning. Go call the doctor, Sister
Marie. Oh, go quickly"

When he came, he too touched her
hand and listened. "She sleeps," he
said, at length. "She may live. Keep
everything profoundly quiet."

Never could Hope forget that vigil.
As the hours passed, and still the exhausted patient slept and slept, some

more than natural strength seemed given to the young watcher, who would not quit the bedside, only taking a cup of milk to sustain her, for how long she never knew.

At last, when the sun had sunk and the first soft shades of night began to fall, Mrs Saville slowly lifted her eyelids and recognised Hope. She smiled gently, as if feeling comfortable and pleased to see her. She was too weak to speak. The relief was too sudden, too delightful, for Hope's self-command. "Oh, thank God! thank God! you are better! you will live! we shall save you!" she exclaimed, while the glad tears dropped from her eyes on the poor, helpless hand which she kissed. Mrs Saville smiled again; her lips moved, as if she tried to say something; then she closed her eyes, and an expression of infinite content stole over her worn face.

CHAPTER XI

HAVING seen the doctor, who paid a late visit to his patient, and heard from him the confirmation of her happy anticipations, Hope left Sister Marie in charge, and at length yielded to the imperative necessity for rest.

What joy it was to wake the next morning and feel that danger was past, and that she had helped to save the cold, stern woman who had buried her heart so deep down under her pride, self-will and arrogance that Hope had nearly despaired of touching it! How sweet it was to return to her post and see the delicate face no longer disfigured by

the dusky, purplish hue so surely indicative of fell disease, but pale and cool,
if worn and thin !

Mrs Saville's eyes were closed, but she
was not asleep. The faint rustle of
Hope's dress as she sat down caught her
attention, and she opened them. Then
she smiled, a soft, kindly smile, such as
Hope had never seen before part her
lips, and she made a slight motion of her
almost transparent hand towards Hope's,
who immediately took it and kissed
it tenderly.

"You are really glad," Mrs Saville
whispered — "really," she sighed, a sort
of contented sigh, and kept her eyes fixed
on her young companion's face, as if it
gave her pleasure to look at her.

The day passed in profound quiet.
The patient slept a great deal, and took
all the nourishment offered her, the rest-

ful, contented expression on her countenance assuring the watchers that all was well.

The afternoon was far advanced when Sister Marie, who had been taking her turn of rest, stood in the doorway and made a sign to Hope, who came to her in the next room.

"A gentleman has arrived and wishes to see you," whispered the Sister.

"What kind of gentleman?" asked Hope, in the same tone.

"He is stout and grey."

"Ah! Mr Rawson!" exclaimed Hope; and she hastened to the *salon*, where she found that gentleman awaiting her. He looked weary and anxious.

"How is she?" he exclaimed, taking both the hands she held out. "Is there any hope?"

"Oh, thank God, she is out of

danger !" she cried, bursting into tears, her nerves no longer able to resist her emotion, now that the terrible strain upon them was removed.

˙ "Thank God indeed! It would have been terrible if she had died unreconciled to her son, for he was really fond of her. They were fonder of each other apart than together. Why, my dear young lady, you look completely worn out. The courier has told me of your devotion. I trust in God you will not suffer for it."

"No, I am sure I shall not. God has given me strength."

"Your—Hugh Saville will thank you and repay you for this." And the good man walked the room, greatly moved.

Hope sat down, and, covering her face with her handkerchief, wept quietly for a few moments; then, resuming her self-control, she began to tell Mr Rawson the story of Mrs Saville's illness from the first seizure to the present.

"I was moving about," said Rawson, "and the news only reached me three days ago. We were at Thun. My daughter and I started at once. She went straight home from Paris, and I came on here. I must write to Hugh. I know he will be shocked at the idea of never seeing his mother in this world."

"You may be sure *I* kept him informed," said Hope. "Even this morning I managed a short letter to convey the joyful news."

"I trust there will be no drawback to her convalescence. I shall remain here for a week or two, until I see all is safe. It has been an awfully trying time for you. Such responsibility; and had she

s

died, that unjust will would have held good."

"It has been destroyed," said Hope. "Mrs Saville told me so. She was going to make another, when this dreadful fever began."

A long, confidential conversation ensued, then Hope left the family solicitor to the care of the courier and returned to her post.

A week later Mrs Saville was able to leave her bed and receive her confidential adviser.

Worn and emaciated though she looked, her aspect was younger than it had been, so greatly was the expression of mouth and eyes softened.

"I am truly rejoiced to see you once more," said Mr Rawson with a kindly twinkle in his eyes.

" You thought you never should, I suppose," murmured Mrs Saville, giving him her hand.

" Indeed, I feared the worst."

" I was very nearly gone. What seemed to kill me most was the doubt whether anybody cared if I lived or died. The last thing I remember distinctly was Miss Desmond's sad, anxious face. It seemed to say that there was one human being who would regret me. The first experience of returning life was her tears of joy at the chance of my recovery. I shall not soon forget that."

" I think she nursed you very devotedly."

"She did. She has saved my life. She has made herself almost a necessity. I have been a hard woman, Mr Rawson, though not unjust, but somehow this girl, who might well be my daughter, suggests to me that there is something beyond justice, and that is equity."

Then they talked as long as Mr Rawson would stay; but he was careful not to exhaust the convalescent.

It was a joyful day when Mrs Saville first ventured into the *salon*, and still more so when she first ventured out. The day before this event her eldest son arrived in hot haste, and, for so undemonstrative a man, showed great joy at finding his mother not only alive, but rapidly recovering, as persons of an untried constitution do, even after so severe a fever. He expressed his warm acknowledgments to Miss Desmond for her devotion, and said the family were under the deepest obligation to her.

Mrs Saville had gained so much strength in the next few days that her son and Mr Rawson decided that they might leave for London, as with Miss Desmond and her maid the invalid could travel safely as soon as the doctor gave his consent.

"She is very eager to return," said Hope to Mr Rawson as they slowly paced the beach in front of the hotel while waiting for the carriage which was to convey him and his travelling companion to the nearest railway-station.

"Yes. Do you know why? She confessed to me last night. The *Vortigern* will be at Plymouth and paid off in about four or five weeks, and I believe she yearns to see and be reconciled to her son; for she said, 'God has been merciful and spared me to correct some great mistakes, and I dare not myself be unforgiving.'"

"Did she say that?" exclaimed Hope. "Oh, I pray God her mood may not change! Do you know I feel so strangely weak and anxious, it seems impossible I can live through another month of anxiety?"

"You have done splendidly so far; you must not break down at the last," said Mr Rawson. "When you return to London you must come to us for a week's complete rest."

"Thank you. You have been a true, good friend. While I am with *you*, I feel that matters will arrange themselves as we wish; but when I am alone, all my courage seems to evaporate. I trust we may be in London within the next three weeks."

"I hope you may, and I believe you will be. Here is the carriage. Let us go in. I suppose Mr Saville is ready. Nothing proved to me his mother's complete restoration so much as her speech about him. 'Let him go away with you, Mr Rawson,' she said; 'if he travels with us he will only be an additional responsibility to Miss Desmond. Richard is incapable of taking care of himself.' She is marvellously toned down by suffering and sympathy; but we cannot expect the Ethiopian to change his skin, nor the leopard his spots, altogether, though one may become a shade lighter and the other have fewer marks."

It was with a thankful heart that Hope Desmond found herself and her charge safely housed in the Stafford Square mansion. Mrs Saville bore the journey well—indeed, better than her companion, whose pale cheeks and heavy eyes bespoke mental and physical exhaustion.

Mrs Saville's usual medical attendant, or rather the medical attendant of the household, for the wiry woman scarcely knew what indisposition meant, awaited her arrival and noticed Miss Desmond's looks.

"If I might offer advice unasked, I would recommend a tonic and some days' complete repose to this young lady," said the polite practitioner. "It seems to me that her nervous system is somewhat over-strained."

"She shall do as you direct," returned Mrs Saville with her usual decision. "I will look to her myself. She has braved horrible infection for me, and has had a large share in saving my life ; therefore I value hers beyond everyone's, except, of course, my sons' Yes, you look frightfully ill, Hope. I cannot have this."

"Perhaps if I went to Miss Rawson for a few days," said Hope with hesitation, "I might gather strength sooner.

Here I shall always want to be up and about."

"You shall be nursed in no other house than this; so, doctor, send in your prescription soon. As for me, I want nothing but good food and occupation."

"You are indeed marvellously well and strong, considering what an illness you have gone through. We have now every reason to hope that you will be spared to your family and friends for many years."

"Much my family and friends care about that special mercy," returned Mrs Saville, with one of her ironical smiles. "Good morning, doctor." And the doctor bowed himself out.

"Thank God, he is gone! I am dying to read my letters," cried Mrs Saville. "Here is a thick one from Mr Rawson." She opened it, and then, growing rather white, exclaimed, "Why, it encloses one from Hugh!" This she read eagerly, and then re-perused it.

"Ah, if I could believe he cares for me!" she said at length. "The letter is like himself, tender yet obstinate. He will be here nearly as soon as this," she went on, her small, thin fingers closing tightly on the paper. "He implores me to let him see his mother's face once more—the mother he has been so near losing. Rawson has evidently told him of my illness. He confesses I had a right to be angry, but reiterates his conviction that he has done well and wisely in securing the sweetest wife man could have."

"You *will* see him, dear Mrs Saville?" cried Hope, with white, parched lips. "You are so good as to think I was of use to you; if you would amply repay

me, see your son—let him plead for his
wife. They *are* married, you cannot
separate them, and if she is a true
woman it will break her heart to
know she has parted mother and son.
It is in your power to confer *such*
happiness."

"I *will* receive my son. As to his
wife, I cannot say what I shall do. I
gave Rawson directions to have her
watched; it was a shabby thing to do,
but I did it. He has had her closely
shadowed, but she has been absolutely
well conducted. Still, if it is in my
power to confer much happiness, it was
in *hers* to create much misery, and
she did it! Why, Hope, what is the
matter? Are you ill?"

Hope fell back in her chair so deadly
white and motionless that Mrs Saville
was terror-struck. She rang violently,

and, rushing to the fainting girl, began to rub her cold hands.

"Bring water, wine! Send Jessop! Call back the doctor!" she cried, in great agitation to the astonished butler, who had never before seen his imperious mistress so moved.

"The doctor has just driven off, 'm; but I will send Jessop."

Soon the lady's-maid, the butler and the housekeeper were trying to bring Miss Desmond back to life. When she did open her eyes they sought Mrs Saville's; she smiled, and feebly put out her hand.

"Now she must go to bed," said Mrs Saville, holding the offered hand in both her own. "She had better be carried upstairs."

"I can walk quite well; at least in a few minutes," murmured Hope, "if Jessop will help me."

Thus Hope was relegated to her own room, where Mrs Saville insisted she must remain all the next day. Wonderful to relate, that lady spent most of it at her bedside, reading or knitting. Neither spoke much, yet they had a certain comfort in the companionship. Miss Rawson called and was admitted during Mrs Saville's absence, when she went for a short airing, which she considered essential for her own health.

To her Hope explained that she must for the present refuse her hospitable invitation. Then they talked long and confidentially, and Miss Rawson took charge of a couple of letters when she bade her young friend good-bye.

It was now established that Miss Desmond was not to appear till luncheon-time, Mrs Saville being content to read the papers herself. The doctor was not quite satisfied; his young patient did not recover strength or tone; she was depressed and nervous, averse from food, sleepless. Some complete change to a bracing place might be necessary. Mrs Saville, who was deeply concerned, went eagerly into the question of localities, but Hope implored, almost piteously, not to be sent away.

It was the end of September, and London was at its emptiest; Mrs Saville was therefore spared the visits and kind inquiries of her kinsfolk and acquaintance. She was ill at ease from anxiety concerning Hope. All that was kindly and grateful in her strong nature had been drawn forth by the desolate orphan girl who had the spirit to withstand her hitherto unresisted tyranny, and the perception to appeal to the better self which lay beneath it.

So Mrs Saville sat by herself, thinking deeply of her past, her present, and the possible future, one warm, rainy morning. "Horrid weather for Hope," she thought; "impossible for nerves to get right under such skyey influence." Yes, she must get Hope out of town. How desolate her life would be without that girl! and she would need comfort and support in coming years. Even if she brought herself to accept Hugh's wife, she would probably turn out a thorn in their side and keep her and her son apart.

Here the old butler, with a beaming face, announced "Mr Hugh, ma'am," and her son entered. How well, how distinguished, he looked! his strong face deeply embrowned, his fine eyes looking eager yet soft.

"Hugh!" cried Mrs Saville, rising, and trembling from head to foot.

"My dear mother!" he returned, tenderly, with the slight hoarseness of warm emotion, and he clasped her in his arms, kissing her affectionately "Are you indeed safe and well?"

"My son! you have nearly broken my heart!" Her tones told him he was already half forgiven.

"Rawson told me this morning, just now, that I might venture to call. You must forgive me, mother. I know I deserved your anger, and this I regret. I only want you to let me come and see you sometimes, and I will trouble you no more. I can fight for my own hand; but you must accept my innocent wife too."

"It will be a hard task, Hugh. I am a prejudiced woman, and my prejudices are strong against *her*."

"I think they will melt when you see her, mother."

"I doubt it," Mrs Saville was begin-ning, when the door opened, and Hope Desmond walked slowly into the room. She seemed very pale and fragile in her simple black dress. No sooner had she caught sight of Hugh than her cheeks flushed, her great brown eyes lit up with a look half joy, half terror, and her lips parted with a slight cry.

Hugh Saville sprang forward, exclaim-ing, "My own love! my own darling wife!" and folded her in a rapturous embrace, kissing her hair, her eyes, her lips, forgetful of everything else.

Mrs Saville again rose from her chair, and stood petrified. At last Hope disen-tangled herself from her husband's arms, and, crossing to where her mother-in-law stood, said brokenly, "Can you forgive me the deceit I have practised? Can you have patience to hear my explanation?"

T

" I am bewildered," cried Mrs Saville, looking from one to the other. " Is Hope Desmond your wife, Hugh ? "

" She is ! Can you not forgive me now ? " said Hugh, advancing to support Hope's trembling form by passing his arm around her.

" It is incredible ! How did you come to impose upon me in this way ? "

" I will tell you all," Hope began, when she was interrupted by a message which the butler brought from Mr Rawson requesting to be admitted.

" Show him up ; he is a party to the fraud," said Mrs Saville, sternly.

Hugh drew his wife closer to him as Mr Rawson entered looking radiant.

" I trust you do not consider me an intruder," he said.

" You come just when you are wanted. I feel my brain turning," returned Mrs Saville.

"If you will listen," urged Hope with clasped hands.

"Yes, pray hear Mrs Hugh Saville," said Mr Rawson.

Mrs Saville turned a startled look upon him, and Hope went on : "When I came to this good friend, who offered me the shelter of his house so soon as he found I was the niece of his old rector, I was in despair. I began to realise the mistake, the disobedience, that Hugh had been guilty of. I had yielded too readily to the temptation of spending my life with him. I felt that I was the cause of his troubles, and I was overwhelmed. I wished that I could die ; anything to be no longer a burden and an obstacle. Then I heard Mr Rawson speak of finding a companion for Mrs Saville, and the thought came to me of being that companion, and perhaps winning her affec-

tion for myself and restoration for Hugh."
A sudden sob interrupted her; then, with
an effort, she went on: "Mr Rawson
was startled at the idea, but his daughter
at once took it up, and, after some
discussion, it was agreed that I should
make the desperate attempt. I was
therefore introduced to you by two of
my names—Hope Desmond. I was called
Katherine Hope Desmond after my
mother, who was Uncle Desmond's only
sister. How I had courage to brave
such an experiment I cannot now understand, for my heart"—she pressed her
hands against her bosom, and, disengaging
herself, made a step nearer her mother-
in-law—"seems to flutter and fail me.
But the desire to retrieve the wrong I
had wrought sustained me. I did not
tell Hugh what I had undertaken until
I had been some weeks with you. He

was much alarmed, and begged me not
to risk too much—to leave as soon as I
could, if the strain was too great; but
he did not forbid me to stay. So I
stayed. How dreadful the beginning
was! Yet, though you were cold and
stern, I could bear it, for you are too
strong to be suspicious, or petty, or
narrow, and I dared not let myself fear
you; and then—I grew to know you
had a heart. That is what makes this
moment so terrible; I fear your dis-
approval more than your displeasure.
Now, can you, will you, forgive me?"

Mrs Saville was silent; her brows were
knit, her eyes downcast; yet Hope dared
to take the fine, small hand which lay
on the arm of the chair. Mrs Saville did
not draw it away. The lookers-on held
their breath. Then she drew Hope's to
her, and gently stroked it. "I think,"

she said slowly, "that you are the only creature that ever understood me. I forgive your husband, and accept you—not because his disobedience is pardonable, but because, when I came back from the jaws of death, the first sight that met my eyes were your tears of joy at my recovery. Yet, had I died intestate, you and your husband would have been far better off than you will be ; and you knew it. You are the first that has ever given me what gold cannot buy "

"Mother," cried Hugh Saville, in a tone of wounded feeling, " I always loved you as much as you would let me."

" Perhaps you did. I believe you did," said his mother.

Hope had sunk on her knees, and kissed the hand which held hers, then her head fell forward, and Hugh sprang forward to lift her.

" She is quite overdone," he exclaimed, almost indignantly. " She is but the ghost of her former self." And he placed her in an easy-chair, where she lay with closed eyes.

" Happiness will be a rapid restorative," said Mrs Saville, kindly. " Now, what punishment is to be dealt out to *you*, traitor that you are ? " she continued, turning to Mr Rawson. " To enter into a conspiracy against your trusting client ! Shall I degrade you from the high office of my chief adviser ? I must hold a council, and the council-board shall be my dinner-table. Bring your daughter to dinner this evening, and we shall settle many matters. And, Hope, if you feel equal to the task, write to Richard, inviting him to dinner to meet his new sister-in-law."

" Very few fellows have so good a right

to be proud of a wife as I have," cried Hugh, exultingly. " Our old naval stories of desperate cutting-out exploits are poor compared to the enduring courage that upheld Kate, as I always call her, through the long strain of her bold undertaking.'

" She has enlightened me, at all events," said Mrs Saville. " Now go away to the drawing-room and have your talk out. The doctor insists that a complete change is necessary for Hope's recovery : so take your wife away to-morrow for your long-delayed honeymoon. But, remember, whenever you are pursuing your profession on the high seas, I claim the companion-ship of Mr Rawson's pleasant *protégée*."

" Dear Mrs Saville, I will be your loving daughter as long as you care to have me near you," cried Hope ; and, no longer hesitating, she folded her formidable mother-in-law in her warm embrace.

THE END.

14 *Bedford Street,*
Strand,
London, W.C.

F. V. WHITE & CO.'S

LIST OF

PUBLICATIONS

AT ALL CIRCULATING LIBRARIES.

A MAGNIFICENT YOUNG MAN. By JOHN STRANGE WINTER, Author of "Bootles' Baby," "A Seventh Child," &c. 1 vol., cloth gilt, bevelled boards. 6s. (4th Edition.) (And at all Booksellers'.)

A RIVERSIDE ROMANCE. By Mrs EDWARD KENNARD. Author of "The Girl in the Brown Habit," "The Catch of the County," &c. 1 vol., bevelled boards. 6s. (And at all Booksellers'.)

A LADY IN BLACK. By FLORENCE WARDEN, Author of "The House on the Marsh," "My Child and I," &c. 1 vol., bevelled boards. 6s. (And at all Booksellers'.)

A WOMAN OF THE COMMUNE. By G. A. HENTY, Author of "All but Lost," "The Curse of Carne's Hold," &c. 1 vol., bevelled boards. 6s. (And at all Booksellers'.)

A SPOILT GIRL. By FLORENCE WARDEN. 1 vol., bevelled boards. 6s. (2d Edition.) (And at all Booksellers'.)

FOOLED BY A WOMAN. By Mrs EDWARD KENNARD. 1 vol., bevelled boards. 6s. (2d Edition.) (And at all Booksellers'.)

A SOUL ASTRAY. By Mrs LOVETT CAMERON, Author of "In a Grass Country," "Jack's Secret," &c. 1 vol., bevelled boards. 6s. (2d Edition.) (And at all Booksellers'.)

A TUG OF WAR. By Mrs HUNGERFORD, Author of "Molly Bawn," "Nora Creina," &c. 1 vol., bevelled boards. 6s. (2d Edition.) (And at all Booksellers'.)

A BAD LOT. By Mrs LOVETT CAMERON, Author of "In a Grass Country," "A Tragic Blunder," &c. 3 vols. 18s.

A GIRL'S FOLLY. By ANNIE THOMAS (Mrs Pender Cudlip), Author of "Allerton Towers," "Eyre of Blendon," &c. 3 vols. 18s.

A RACING RUBBER. By HAWLEY SMART, Author of "Breezie Langton," "Beatrice and Benedick," &c. 2 vols. 12s.

A PERFECT FOOL. By FLORENCE WARDEN, Author of "The House on the Marsh," "My Child and I," &c. 2 vols. 12s.

A BLAMELESS WOMAN. By the same Author. 1 vol., cloth gilt, bevelled boards. 6s. (3d Edition.) (And at all Booksellers'.)

A BORN SOLDIER. By the same Author. 1 vol., cloth gilt, bevelled boards. 6s. (And at all Booksellers'.)

THE WORKS OF JOHN STRANGE WINTER.

UNIFORM IN STYLE AND PRICE.

(At all Booksellers' and Bookstalls.)   In Paper Covers, 1s.; Cloth, 1s. 6d. each.

I MARRIED A WIFE. (Profusely Illustrated.) (2d Edition.)

PRIVATE TINKER, and Other Stories. (Profusely Illustrated. (3d Edition.)

THE MAJOR'S FAVOURITE. (2d Edition.)

THE STRANGER WOMAN. (3d Edition.)

RED COATS. (Profusely Illustrated.) (5th Edition.)

A MAN'S MAN. (4th Edition.)

THAT MRS SMITH. (2d Edition.)

THREE GIRLS. (4th Edition.)

MERE LUCK. (3d Edition.)

LUMLEY THE PAINTER. (3d Edition.)

GOOD-BYE. (8th Edition.)

HE WENT FOR A SOLDIER. (8th Edition.)

FERRERS COURT (7th Edition.)

BUTTONS. (8th Edition.)

A LITTLE FOOL. (11th Edition.)

MY POOR DICK. (10th Edition.) Illustrated by MAURICE GREIFFENHAGEN.

BOOTLES' CHILDREN. (12th Edition.) Illustrated by J. BERNARD PARTRIDGE.

"John Strange Winter is never more thoroughly at home than when delineating the characters of children, and everyone will be delighted with the dignified Madge and the quaint Pearl. The book is mainly occupied with the love affairs of Terry (the soldier servant who appears in many of the preceding books), but the children buzz in and out of its pages much as they would come in and out of a room in real life, pervading and brightening the house in which they dwell."—*Leicester Daily Post*.

THE CONFESSIONS OF A PUBLISHER.

"The much discussed question of the relations between a publisher and his clients furnishes Mr John Strange Winter with material for one of the brightest tales of the season. Abel Drinkwater's autobiography is written from a humorous point of view ; yet here, as elsewhere, 'many a true word is spoken in jest,' and in the conversations of the publisher and his too ingenuous son, facts come to light that are worthy of the attention of aspirants to literary fame."—*Morning Post*.

MIGNON'S HUSBAND. (15th Edition.)

"It is a capital love story, full of high spirits, and written in a dashing style and will charm the most melancholy of readers into hearty enjoyment of its fun."—*Scotsman*.

THAT IMP. (13th Edition.)

"Barrack life is abandoned for the nonce, and the author of 'Bootles' Baby' introduces readers to a country home replete with every comfort and containing men and women whose acquaintanceship we can only regret can never blossom into friendship."—*Whitehall Review*.

"This charming little book is bright and breezy, and has the ring of supreme truth about it."—*Vanity Fair*.

MIGNON'S SECRET. (18th Edition.)

"In 'Mignon's Secret' Mr Winter has supplied a continuation to the never-to-be-forgotten 'Bootles' Baby.' The story is gracefully and touchingly told."—*John Bull*.

F. V. WHITE & Co., 14 Bedford Street, Strand.

ON MARCH. (10th Edition.)

"This short story is characterised by Mr Winter's customary truth in detail, humour, and pathos."—*Academy.*

"By publishing 'On March,' Mr J. S. Winter has added another little gem to his well-known store of regimental sketches. The story is written with humour and a deal of feeling."—*Army and Navy Gazette.*

IN QUARTERS. (12th Edition.)

"'In Quarters' is one of those rattling tales of soldiers' life which the public have learned to thoroughly appreciate."—*The Graphic.*

"The author of 'Bootles' Baby' gives us here another story of military life, which few have better described."—*British Quarterly Review.*

ARMY SOCIETY: Life in a Garrison Town.

Cloth, gilt, 6s. ; in Picture Boards, 2s. (10th Edition.)

"This discursive story, dealing with life in a garrison town, is full of pleasant 'go' and movement which has distinguished 'Bootles' Baby,' 'Pluck,' or, in fact, a majority of some half-dozen novelettes which the author has submitted to the eyes of railway bookstall patronisers."—*Daily Telegraph.*

"The strength of the book lies in its sketches of life in a garrison town, which are undeniably clever. It is pretty clear that Mr Winter draws from life."—*St James's Gazette.*

GARRISON GOSSIP, Gathered in Blankhampton.

(A Sequel to "ARMY SOCIETY.") Cloth, 2s. 6d. ; Picture Boards, 2s. (6th Edition.)

"'Garrison Gossip' may fairly rank with 'Cavalry Life,' and the various other books with which Mr Winter has so agreeably beguiled our leisure hours."—*Saturday Review.*

"The novel fully maintains the reputation which its author has been fortunate enough to gain in a special line of his own."—*Graphic.*

A SIEGE BABY. (5th Edition.)

Cloth, 2s. 6d. ; Picture Boards, 2s.

"The story which gives its title to this new sheaf of stories by the popular author of 'Bootles' Baby' is a very touching and pathetic one. . Amongst the other stories, the one entitled 'Out of the Mists' is, perhaps, the best written, although the tale of true love it embodies comes to a most melancholy ending."—*County Gentleman.*

BEAUTIFUL JIM. (9th Edition.)

Cloth, 2s. 6d. ; Picture Boards, 2s.

MRS BOB. (7th Edition.)

Cloth, 2s. 6d. ; Picture Boards, 2s.

THE OTHER MAN'S WIFE. (6th Edition.)

Cloth, 2s. 6d. Picture Boards, 2s.

MY GEOFF ; or, The Experiences of a Lady Help. (6th Edition.) Cloth, 2s. 6d. ; Picture Boards, 2s.

ONLY HUMAN. (5th Edition.) Cloth, 2s. 6d. ; Picture Boards, 2s.

AUNT JOHNNIE. (4th Edition.) Cloth, 2s. 6d. ; Picture Boards, 2s.

THE SOUL OF THE BISHOP. (5th Edit.) Cloth, 2s. 6d.; Picture Boards, 2s.

A SEVENTH CHILD. (5th Edition.) Cloth, 2s. 6d. ; Picture Boards, 2s.

A BORN SOLDIER. Cloth gilt, Bevelled Boards, 6s. Cloth, 2s. 6d. (2d Edition.)

A BLAMELESS WOMAN. (A New Novel.) 3d Edition.

Cloth gilt, Bevelled Boards, 6s.

A MAGNIFICENT YOUNG MAN. (A New Novel.) Cloth gilt. Bevelled Boards. 6s. (4th Edition.)

NOVELS BY HAWLEY SMART.
(At all Booksellers' and Bookstalls.)
A RACING RUBBER. Cloth gilt, 2s. 6d.

BEATRICE AND BENEDICK : A Romance of the Crimea.
Cloth, 2s. 6d. ; Picture Boards, 2s. (2d Edition.)

THE PLUNGER. Cloth gilt, 2s. 6d. ; Picture Bds., 2s. (6th Edit.)

LONG ODDS. Cloth gilt, 2s. 6d. ; Picture Boards, 2s. (5th Edit.)

THE MASTER OF RATHKELLY. Cloth, 2s. 6d. ; Picture
Boards, 2s. (5th Edition.)

THE OUTSIDER. Cl. gilt, 2s. 6d. Picture Bds., 2s. (8th Edit.)

By the same Author. In Paper Covers, 1s.; Cloth, 1s. 6d.

VANITY'S DAUGHTER.

THRICE PAST THE POST. (Cloth, 1s. 6d. only)

BY G. A. HENTY.
(At all Libraries and Booksellers'.)
A WOMAN OF THE COMMUNE. Bevelled boards, 6s.

BY MRS OLIPHANT.
(At all Booksellers' and Bookstalls.)
THE SORCERESS. Cloth, 3s. 6d. ; Picture Boards, 2s.

NOVELS BY B. L. FARJEON.
(At all Booksellers' and Bookstalls.) Cloth, 2s. 6d. ; Picture Boards, 2s.

THE MARCH OF FATE.

BASIL AND ANNETTE. (2d Edition.)

A YOUNG GIRL'S LIFE. (3d Edition.)

TOILERS OF BABYLON. (2d Edition.)

THE DUCHESS OF ROSEMARY LANE. (2d Edition.)
In Paper Covers, 1s. Cloth, 1s. 6d.

THE PERIL OF RICHARD PARDON. (2d Edition.)

A STRANGE ENCHANTMENT.

A VERY YOUNG COUPLE.

NOVELS BY B. M. CROKER.
(At all Booksellers' and Bookstalls.)
A THIRD PERSON. Cloth, 2s. 6d.; Picture Bds., 2s.

INTERFERENCE. (3d Edit.) Cloth, 2s. 6d.; Picture Bds., 2s.

TWO MASTERS. (3d Edition.) Cloth, 2s. 6d.; Picture Bds., 2s.

NOVELS BY HELEN MATHERS.
(At all Booksellers' and Bookstalls.)
A MAN OF TO-DAY. Cloth, 2s. 6d.
In Paper Covers, 1s. ; Cloth, 1s. 6d. each.

WHAT THE GLASS TOLD. | T'OTHER DEAR CHARMER.

A STUDY OF A WOMAN ; OR, VENUS VICTRIX.

Sir RANDAL H. ROBERTS, Bart.'s, Sporting Novels

(At all Booksellers' and Bookstalls.)
HANDICAPPED. (A New Novel.) Cloth gilt, 2s. 6d.
NOT IN THE BETTING. Cloth gilt, 2s. 6d.
CURB AND SNAFFLE. Cloth gilt, 2s. 6d.

NOVELS BY MRS ALEXANDER FRASER.

(At all Booksellers' and Bookstalls.)
A MODERN BRIDEGROOM. (3d Edition.) Cloth, 2s. 6d. ; Picture Boards, 2s.
DAUGHTERS OF BELGRAVIA. Cloth, 2s. 6d. ; Picture Boards, 2s.
SHE CAME BETWEEN. Cloth, 2s. 6d.

NOVELS BY MRS LOVETT CAMERON.

(At all Booksellers' and Bookstalls.)
A SOUL ASTRAY. Cloth (Bevelled Boards), 6s. (2d Edition.)
LITTLE LADY LEE. (A New Novel.) Cloth, 2s. 6d.
A BAD LOT. Cloth, 2s. 6d.
A TRAGIC BLUNDER. Cloth, 2s. 6d.
A BACHELOR'S BRIDAL. Cloth, 2s. 6d.; Picture Boards, 2s.
A SISTER'S SIN. Cloth, 2s. 6d. ; Picture Boards, 2s.
IN A GRASS COUNTRY. A Story of Love and Sport. (10th
   Edition.) Cl. gilt, 2s. 6d.; Picture Boards, 2s.; Paper Covers, 1s.
WEAK WOMAN. (3d Edition.) Cloth, 2s. 6d. ; Picture Boards, 2s.
JACK'S SECRET. (3d Edition.) Cloth, 2s. 6d.; Picture Boards, 2s.
A LOST WIFE. (3d Edition.) Cloth, 2s. 6d.; Picture Boards, 2s.
A DAUGHTER'S HEART. Cloth, 2s. 6d. ; Picture Boards, 2s.
THE MAN WHO DIDN'T. (2d Ed.) Paper Covers, 1s. ; Cl., 1s. 6d.

NOVELS BY MRS HUNGERFORD.

(Author of "Molly Bawn.") (At all Booksellers' and Bookstalls.)
A TUG OF WAR. Cloth (Bevelled Boards), 6s. (2d Edition.)
PETER'S WIFE. (2d Edition.) Cloth, 2s. 6d.   [Boards, 2s.
AN UNSATISFACTORY LOVER. (2d Ed.) Cl., 2s. 6d. ; Picture
NORA CREINA. Cloth, 2s. 6d. ; Picture Boards, 2s.
LADY PATTY ; A Sketch. (3d Edition.) Cl., 2s. 6d. ; Picture Bds., 2s.
APRIL'S LADY. (4th Edition.) Cloth, 2s. 6d. ; Picture Boards, 2s.
THE HON. MRS VEREKER. (4th Edition.) Cloth, 2s. 6d. ;
   Picture Boards, 2s.
A MAD PRANK. Paper Covers. 1s. ; Cloth, 1s. 6d.
A CONQUERING HEROINE. Paper Covers, 1s. ; Cloth, 1s. 6d.

By JUSTIN M'CARTHY, M.P., and Mrs CAMPBELL PRAED.

(Authors of "The Right Honourable," &c.)
(At all Booksellers' and Bookstalls.)
THE LADIES' GALLERY. (2d Edition.) Cloth, 2s. 6d.; Picture
   Boards, 2s.
THE RIVAL PRINCESS ; a London Romance of To-day. (3d Edit.)
   Cloth, 2s. 6d. ; Picture Boards, 2s.

BY MRS CAMPBELL PRAED.

(At all Booksellers' and Bookstalls.)
THE ROMANCE OF A CHÂLET. Cl., 2s. 6d. ; Picture Bds. 2s.

BY MRS J. H. RIDDELL.

(At all Booksellers' and Bookstalls.)
A SILENT TRAGEDY. Paper Covers, 1s.; Cloth, 1s. 6d.

F. V. WHITE & Co., 14 Bedford Street, Strand.

NOVELS BY MRS ALEXANDER.
(At all Booksellers' and Bookstalls.)

A CHOICE OF EVILS. (2d Edition.) Cloth, 2s. 6d.
WHAT GOLD CANNOT BUY. (3d Edition.) Cloth, 2s. 6d. ; Picture Boards, 2s.
FOUND WANTING. Cloth, 2s. 6d.; Picture Boards, 2s.
FOR HIS SAKE. Cloth, 2s. 6d. ; Picture Boards, 2s.
A WOMAN'S HEART. Cloth, 2s. 6d. : Picture Boards, 2s.
BLIND FATE. Cloth, 2s 6d.; Picture Boards, 2s.
BY WOMAN'S WIT. (7th Edition.) Picture Cover, 1s.
WELL WON. Cloth, 1s. 6d. only.

NOVELS BY HUME NISBET.
(At all Booksellers' and Bookstalls.)

THE GREAT SECRET: A Tale of To-morrow. Cloth, 2s 6d.
A DESERT BRIDE: A Story of Adventure in India and Persia. With Illustrations by the Author. Cloth, 3s. 6d. ; also in Picture Boards, 2s, (2d Edition.)
A SINGULAR CRIME. In Paper Covers, 1s.; Cloth, 1s. 6d.
A BUSH GIRL'S ROMANCE. With Illustrations by the Author. Cloth, 3s. 6d. also in Picture Boards, 2s. (2d Edition.)
THE HAUNTED STATION, and other Stories. With Illustrations by the Author. Cloth gilt, 2s. 6d.
THE QUEEN'S DESIRE ; A Romance of the Indian Mutiny. With Illustrations by the Author. Cloth, 3s. 6d. ; Picture Boards, 2s.
THE BUSHRANGER'S SWEETHEART: An Australian Romance. Picture Boards, 2s. (5th Edition.)
THE SAVAGE QUEEN: A Romance of the Natives of Van Dieman's Land. Cloth, 2s. 6d. ; Picture Boards, 2s. (3d Edition.)

NOVELS BY FLORENCE WARDEN.
At all Booksellers' and Bookstalls.)   [Booksellers'.)

A LADY IN BLACK. 1 vol. Bevelled Boards, 6s. (At all Libraries and
A SPOILT GIRL. (2d Edition.) Bevelled Boards, 6s. (At all Libraries and Booksellers'.)   [Booksellers'.)
KITTY'S ENGAGEMENT. Bevelled Boards, 6s. (At all Libraries and
A PERFECT FOOL. Cloth, 2s. 6d.
STRICTLY INCOG.: Being the Record of a Passage through Bohemia. Cloth, 2s. 6d.
MY CHILD AND I: A Woman's Story. Cloth, 2s. 6d. ; Picture Boards, 2s.
A YOUNG WIFE'S TRIAL; or, Ralph Ryder of Brent. Cloth, 2s. 6d.; Picture Boards, 2s
A WILD WOOING. Cloth, 2s. 6d.: Picture Boards, 2s.
A WITCH OF THE HILLS. (3d Edition.) Cloth, 2s. 6d.; Picture Boards, 2s.
A WOMAN'S FACE. Picture Boards, 2s.
THE WOMAN WITH THE DIAMONDS. Paper Covers, 1s. ; Cloth, 1s. 6d.
A SCARBOROUGH ROMANCE: The Strange Story of Mary Glynde. Paper Covers, 1s.; Cloth, 1s. 6d.
GRAVE LADY JANE Paper Covers, 1s.; Cloth, 1s. 6d.
A SHOCK TO SOCIETY (3d Edition.) Cloth, 1s. 6d. only.
CITY AND SUBURBAN. (2d Edition.) Paper Covers, 1s.; Cloth, 1s. 6d.

NOVELS BY "RITA."
(At all Booksellers' and Bookstalls.)

THE ENDING OF MY DAY: The Story of a Stormy Life. Cloth, 2s. 6d. ; Picture Boards, 2s.
NAUGHTY MRS GORDON : A Romance of Society. In Paper Covers, 1s. ; Cloth, 1s. 6d.
SHEBA: A Study of Girlhood. (5th Edition.) Cloth, 2s. 6d.; Picture Boards, 2s.
THE COUNTESS PHARAMOND. A Sequel to "Sheba." Cloth, 2s. 6d. ; Picture Boards, 2s.
THE MAN IN POSSESSION. Cloth, 2s. 6d. ; Picture Boards, 2s.
THE LAIRD O' COCKPEN. Cloth, 2s. 6d. ; Picture Boards, 2s.
MISS KATE. (4th Edition.) Cloth, 2s. 6d. ; Picture Boards, 2s.
THE SEVENTH DREAM. 1s. and 1s. 6d.
THE DOCTOR'S SECRET. (2d Edition) 1s. and 1s 6d.

ONE VOLUME NOVELS BY POPULAR AUTHORS.

Crown 8vo, Cloth, 2s. 6d. each.   (At all Booksellers' and Bookstalls.)

By JOHN STRANGE WINTER.

A BORN SOLDIER. | A SEVENTH CHILD. | MRS BOB.
THE OTHER MAN'S WIFE. | THE SOUL OF THE BISHOP.
AUNT JOHNNIE. | ONLY HUMAN. | MY GEOFF.
GARRISON GOSSIP. | A SIEGE BABY. | BEAUTIFUL JIM.

By MRS EDWARD KENNARD.

THE CATCH OF THE COUNTY.
THE PLAYTHING OF AN HOUR, and other Stories. (A New Work)
THE HUNTING GIRL. | WEDDED TO SPORT. (3s. 6d.)
JUST LIKE A WOMAN. | KILLED IN THE OPEN.
SPORTING TALES. (A New Work.) | TWILIGHT TALES (Illus.).
THAT PRETTY LITTLE HORSE-BREAKER.
A HOMBURG BEAUTY. | A CRACK COUNTY.
MATRON OR MAID? | A REAL GOOD THING.
LANDING A PRIZE. | STRAIGHT AS A DIE.
THE GIRL IN THE BROWN HABIT.
OUR FRIENDS IN THE HUNTING-FIELD.

By HAWLEY SMART.

A RACING RUBBER. | THE PLUNGER.
BEATRICE AND BENEDICK. | LONG ODDS.
THE MASTER OF RATHKELLY. | THE OUTSIDER.

By HELEN MATHERS.   By MRS CAMPBELL PRAED.

A MAN OF TO-DAY. | THE ROMANCE OF A CHÂLET.

By B. L. FARJEON.

THE MARCH OF FATE. | A YOUNG GIRL'S LIFE.
TOILERS OF BABYLON. | BASIL AND ANNETTE.
THE DUCHESS OF ROSEMARY LANE.

By MAY CROMMELIN.

THE FREAKS OF LADY FORTUNE.

By FLORENCE WARDEN.

A PERFECT FOOL. | A WILD WOOING.
STRICTLY INCOG : Being the Record of a Passage through Bohemia.
MY CHILD AND I. | A WITCH OF THE HILLS.
A YOUNG WIFE'S TRIAL ; or, Ralph Ryder of Brent.

By MABEL COLLINS.   By MRS OLIPHANT.

VIOLA FANSHAWE. | THE SORCERESS. (3s. 6d.)

By B. M. CROKER.

A THIRD PERSON. | TWO MASTERS. | INTERFERENCE.

By HUME NISBET.

THE GREAT SECRET. (A New Novel.) | THE SAVAGE QUEEN.
THE QUEEN'S DESIRE. (3s. 6d.) | A DESERT BRIDE. (3s. 6d.)
A BUSH GIRL'S ROMANCE. (3s. 6d.)
THE HAUNTED STATION, and other Stories.

By ALAN ST AUBYN.

IN THE SWEET WEST COUNTRY. (A New Novel.)
A TRAGIC HONEYMOON.

By SIR RANDAL H. ROBERTS, Bart.

HANDICAPPED. (A New Novel.)
NOT IN THE BETTING. | CURB AND SNAFFLE.

ONE VOLUME NOVELS—*Continued.*

By AMYE READE (Author of "Ruby," &c.)
SLAVES OF THE SAWDUST. A Story of Acrobat Life.

By F. C. PHILIPS and C. J. WILLS.
SYBIL ROSS'S MARRIAGE.

By MRS ALEXANDER.

WHAT GOLD CANNOT BUY.	A WOMAN'S HEART.
A CHOICE OF EVILS.	FOUND WANTING.
BLIND FATE.	FOR HIS SAKE.

By MRS LOVETT CAMERON.

LITTLE LADY LEE. (A New Novel.)	A BAD LOT.
A TRAGIC BLUNDER.	A BACHELOR'S BRIDAL.
A SISTER'S SIN.	A LOST WIFE.
IN A GRASS COUNTRY.	A DAUGHTER'S HEART.
JACK'S SECRET.	WEAK WOMAN.

By JUSTIN M'CARTHY, M.P., and Mrs CAMPBELL PRAED.

THE RIVAL PRINCESS.	THE LADIES' GALLERY.

By MRS ROBERT JOCELYN.

THE M.F.H.'S DAUGHTER.	DRAWN BLANK.
THE CRITON HUNT MYSTERY.	A BIG STAKE.
ONLY A HORSE-DEALER.	FOR ONE SEASON ONLY.

By BRET HARTE.
THE CRUSADE OF THE "EXCELSIOR."

By the Hon. MRS FETHERSTONHAUGH.
DREAM FACES.

By FERGUS HUME.
WHOM GOD HATH JOINED. | THE MAN WITH A SECRET.

By MRS HUNGERFORD (Author of "Molly Bawn").

PETER'S WIFE.

THE HON. MRS VEREKER.	APRIL'S LADY.
NORA CREINA.	LADY PATTY.

AN UNSATISFACTORY LOVER.

By "RITA."

THE ENDING OF MY DAY.	SHEBA.
THE COUNTESS PHARAMOND.	A Sequel to "Sheba."
THE MAN IN POSSESSION.	MISS KATE.
THE LAIRD O' COCKPEN.	

By MRS ALEXANDER FRASER.

A MODERN BRIDEGROOM.	SHE CAME BETWEEN.
DAUGHTERS OF BELGRAVIA.	

By FLORENCE MARRYAT.
MY SISTER, THE ACTRESS. | HER WORLD AGAINST A LIE.

By MAY CROMMELIN and J. MORAY BROWN.
VIOLET VYVIAN, M.F.H.

By F. C. PHILIPS and PERCY FENDALL.

A DAUGHTER'S SACRIFICE.	MARGARET BYNG.
MY FACE IS MY FORTUNE.	

By HARRIETT JAY.
A MARRIAGE OF CONVENIENCE.

Picture Boards, 2s. each.   At all Booksellers' and Bookstalls.

A SEVENTH CHILD. (5th Edition). By JOHN STRANGE WINTER.
THE SOUL OF THE BISHOP. (5th Edit.) By the same Author.
AUNT JOHNNIE. (4th Edition.) By the same Author.
ONLY HUMAN. (5th Edition.) By the same Author.
MY GEOFF. (6th Edition.) By the same Author.
THE OTHER MAN'S WIFE. (6th Edition.) By the same Author.
MRS BOB. (7th Edition.) By the same Author.
BEAUTIFUL JIM. (9th Edition.) By the same Author.
A SIEGE BABY. (5th Edition.) By the same Author.
GARRISON GOSSIP. (6th Edition.) By the same Author.
ARMY SOCIETY. Life in a Garrison Town. (10th Edition.) By
    the same Author.   [FENDALL.
MY FACE IS MY FORTUNE. By F. C. PHILIPS and PERCY
A DAUGHTER'S SACRIFICE. (3d Ed.) By the same Authors.
THE SORCERESS. By Mrs OLIPHANT.
THE MAN WITH A SECRET. (3d Edition.) By FERGUS HUME.
WHOM GOD HATH JOINED ; a Question of Marriage. (3d
    Edition.) By the same Author.
LONG ODDS. (5th Edition.) By HAWLEY SMART.
THE PLUNGER. (6th Edition.) By the same Author.
THE MASTER OF RATHKELLY. (5th Edit.) By the same Author.
BEATRICE AND BENEDICK. (2d Edit.) By the same Author.
THE OUTSIDER. (8th Edition.) By the same Author.
A BACHELOR'S BRIDAL. By Mrs LOVETT CAMERON.
A LOST WIFE. (3d Edition.) By the same Author.
A DAUGHTER'S HEART. By the same Author.
A SISTER'S SIN. By the same Author.
WEAK WOMAN. (3d Edition.) By the same Author.
IN A GRASS COUNTRY. (10th Edition.) By the same Author.
JACK'S SECRET. (3d Edition.) By the same Author.
WHAT GOLD CANNOT BUY. (3d Edition.) By Mrs ALEXANDER.
FOUND WANTING. By the same Author.
FOR HIS SAKE. By the same Author.
A WOMAN'S HEART. By the same Author.
BLIND FATE. By the same Author.
AN UNSATISFACTORY LOVER. (2d Edit.) By Mrs HUNGERFORD.
THE HON. MRS VEREKER. (4th Edit.) By the same Author.
NORA CREINA. By the same Author.
LADY PATTY. (3d Edition.) By the same Author.
APRIL'S LADY. (4th Edition.) By the same Author.
THE HUNTING GIRL. By Mrs EDWARD KENNARD.
JUST LIKE A WOMAN. By the same Author
WEDDED TO SPORT. By the same Author.
LANDING A PRIZE. (7th Edition.) By the same Author.
THAT PRETTY LITTLE HORSE-BREAKER. (4th Edition.)
    By the same Author.
A HOMBURG BEAUTY. (3d Edition.) By the same Author.
MATRON OR MAID ? (4th Edition.) By the same Author.
A CRACK COUNTY. (6th Edition.) By the same Author.
A REAL GOOD THING. (8th Edition.) By the same Author.
STRAIGHT AS A DIE. (9th Edition.) By the same Author.
THE GIRL IN THE BROWN HABIT. (8th Ed.) By same Author.
OUR FRIENDS IN THE HUNTING-FIELD. By the same Author
KILLED IN THE OPEN. (9th Edition.) By the same Author.

ONE SHILLING NOVELS.

(In Paper Covers). Cloth, 1s. 6d.

(AT ALL BOOKSELLERS' AND BOOKSTALLS.)

I MARRIED A WIFE. By JOHN STRANGE WINTER. Author of "Bootles' Baby," &c. (Profusely Illustrated.) (2d. Edition.)

PRIVATE TINKER, and other Stories. By the same Author. (Profusely Illustrated.) (3d Edition.)

THE MAJOR'S FAVOURITE. (2d Edition.) By the same Author. [same Author.

THE STRANGER WOMAN. (3d Edition.) By the

RED COATS. (Profusely Illustrated.) (5th Edition.) By the same Author.

A MAN'S MAN. (4th Edition.) By the same Author.

THAT MRS SMITH. (2d Edition.) By the same Author.

THREE GIRLS. (4th Edition.) By the same Author.

MERE LUCK. (3d Edition.) By the same Author.

LUMLEY THE PAINTER. (3d Edition.) By the same Author.

GOOD-BYE. (8th Edition.) By the same Author.

HE WENT FOR A SOLDIER. (8th Edition.) By the same Author.

FERRERS COURT. (7th Edition.) By the same Author.

BUTTONS. (8th Edition.) By the same Author.

A LITTLE FOOL. (11th Edition.) By the same Author.

MY POOR DICK. (Illustrated by MAURICE GREIFFEN-HAGEN.) (10th Edition.) By the same Author.

BOOTLES' CHILDREN. (Illustrated by J. BERNARD PARTRIDGE.) (12th Edition.) By the same Author.

THE CONFESSIONS OF A PUBLISHER. By the same Author. [Author.

MIGNON'S HUSBAND. (15th Edition.) By the same

THAT IMP. (13th Edition.) By the same Author.

MIGNON'S SECRET. (18th Edition.) By the same Author.

ON MARCH. (10th Edition.) By the same Author.

IN QUARTERS. (12th Edition.) By the same Author.

A DEVIL IN NUN'S VEILING. By F. C. PHILIPS.

A FRENCH MARRIAGE. By the same Author.

THE INVESTIGATIONS OF JOHN PYM. By DAVID CHRISTIE MURRAY. [CAMERON.

THE MAN WHO DIDN'T. (2d Edit.) By Mrs LOVETT

IN A GRASS COUNTRY. A Story of Love and Sport. (9th Edition.) By the same Author.

A SINGULAR CRIME. By HUME NISBET, Author of "A Bush Girl's Romance," &c. [By FERGUS HUME.

THE GENTLEMAN WHO VANISHED. (2d Edition.)

MISS MEPHISTOPHELES, a Sequel to "Madame Midas." By the same Author. (In Paper Covers only.)

THE PICCADILLY PUZZLE. By Fergus Hume.

THE POWER OF AN EYE. By Mrs Frank St Clair Grimwood, Author of "My Three Years in Manipur."

A VERY YOUNG COUPLE. By B. L. Farjeon, Author of "Toilers of Babylon," &c.

THE PERIL OF RICHARD PARDON. (2d Edition.) By the same Author.

A STRANGE ENCHANTMENT. By the same Author.

A SILENT TRAGEDY. By Mrs J. H. Riddell, Author of "George Geith of Fen Court," &c.

THE MYSTERY OF No. 13. (2d Edition.) By Helen Mathers, Author of "Comin' Thro' the Rye," &c.

WHAT THE GLASS TOLD. By the same Author.

A STUDY OF A WOMAN ; or, Venus Victrix. By the same Author. [(Cloth only.)

MY JO, JOHN. (2d Edition.) By the same Author.

T'OTHER DEAR CHARMER. By the same Author.

BY WOMAN'S WIT. (7th Edition.) By Mrs Alexander. (Paper Covers only.) [(Cloth only.)

WELL WON. By the same Author. (2d Edition.)

TOM'S WIFE. By Lady Margaret Majendie, Author of "Fascination," "Sisters-in-Law," &c.

THE CONFESSIONS OF A DOOR MAT. By Alfred C. Calmour, Author of "The Amber Heart," &c.

THE MYSTERY OF A WOMAN'S HEART. By Mrs Edward Kennard.

THE WOMAN WITH THE DIAMONDS. By Florence Warden. [Author.

CITY AND SUBURBAN. (2d Edition.) By the same

A SCARBOROUGH ROMANCE; the Strange Story of Mary Glynde. By the same Author.

GRAVE LADY JANE. By the same Author.

A SHOCK TO SOCIETY. (3d Edition.) By the same Author. ["Rita."

NAUGHTY MRS GORDON ; a Romance of Society. By

THE DOCTOR'S SECRET. (2d Edition.) By the same Author.

THE SEVENTH DREAM. By the same Author.

VANITY'S DAUGHTER. By Hawley Smart.

THRICE PAST THE POST. By the same Author (Cloth only.)

A CONQUERING HEROINE. By Mrs Hungerford, Author of "Molly Bawn," &c.

A MAD PRANK. By the same Author.

FACING THE FOOTLIGHTS. By Florence Marryat.

DEVIL'S FORD. By Bret Harte. (In Paper Covers only.)